Rhythm & Rhyme

Literacy Time

Level 3

Authors

Timothy Rasinski, Ph.D.

Gay Fawcett, Ph.D.

Karen McGuigan Brothers

SHELL EDUCATION

Standards
For information on how this resource meets national and other state standards, see pages 140–142. You may also review this information by scanning the QR code or visiting our website at http://www.shelleducation.com and following the on-screen directions.

Publishing Credits

Corinne Burton, M.A.Ed., *President*; Emily R. Smith, M.A.Ed., *Editorial Director*; Jennifer Wilson, *Editor*; Evelyn Garcia, M.A.Ed., *Editor*; Grace Alba, *Multimedia Designer*; Don Tran, *Production Artist*; Stephanie Loureiro, *Assistant Editor*; Amber Goff, *Editorial Assistant*

Image Credits

Dreamstime p. 10, p. 62, p. 65, p. 69, p. 110, p. 112, p. 116; iStock p. 5, p. 6, p. 8, p. 11, p. 14, p. 15, p. 17, p. 18, p. 20, p. 27, p. 28, p. 28, p. 29, p. 32, p. 33, p. 34, p. 35, p. 36, p. 37, p. 41, p. 42, p. 43, p. 44, p. 45, p. 47, p. 49, p. 51, p. 55, p. 61, p. 64, p. 69, pp. 70–73, pp. 75–78, p. 81, p. 82, p. 85, p. 89, p. 91, p. 93, pp. 95–98, pp. 100–102, p. 106, p. 108, p. 122, p. 124, p. 127, pp. 130–133, p. 135; all other images Shutterstock

Standards

© Copyright 2010. National Governors Association Center for Best Practices and Council of Chief State School Officers. All rights reserved.

Shell Education
5301 Oceanus Drive
Huntington Beach, CA 92649-1030
http://www.shelleducation.com
ISBN 978-1-4258-1339-0
© 2015 Shell Educational Publishing, Inc.

Table of Contents

Poetry and Literacy

"Reading should not be presented to children as a chore or duty. It should be offered to them as a precious gift."

—Kate DiCamillo

What better gift to give students than fun rhymes to read in order to build literacy skills? Did you grow up singing a song of sixpence, hoping the kittens would find their mittens, and wondering why Georgie Porgie wouldn't leave those little girls alone? We did, along with generations of children. Mother Goose nursery rhymes have helped children achieve literacy since at least the 18th century. Today, we find that many of our children are missing out on nursery rhymes and poetry. Over the years, poetry and rhymes have been called the "neglected component" and "forgotten genre" in our homes and in our school literacy curricula (Denman 1988; Gill 2011; Perfect 1999). Many teachers think that is a shame, and we heartily agree!

There is a growing chorus of scholars who are advocating the return of poetry and poetry lessons in the classroom (Rasinski, Rupley, and Nichols 2012; Seitz 2013). Moreover, there is a growing body of classroom and clinical research demonstrating the power of poetry in growing readers (Iwasaki, Rasinski, Yildirim, and Zimmerman 2013; Rasinski, Rupley, and Nichols 2008; Zimmerman and Rasinski 2012; Rasinski and Zimmerman 2013; Zimmerman, Rasinski, and Melewski 2013). The following information describes the benefits of using poetry and rhyme to enhance literacy skills in the classroom.

Phonological Awareness

Rhymes provide the context for developing phonological awareness. Dunst, Meter, and Hornby (2011) reviewed twelve studies that examined the relationship between nursery rhymes and emergent literacy skills in more than 5,000 children. All of the studies pointed to a relationship between early knowledge of nursery rhymes and phonological awareness, which is a strong predictor of early reading acquisition (Adams 1990; Ball and Blachman 1991; Griffith and Klesius 1990; Templeton and Bear 2011). In fact, one literacy expert, Keith Stanovich, claims phonological awareness as a predictor of reading success is "better than anything else we know of, including I.Q." (Stanovich 1994, 284). Rhymes provide an opportunity for children to play with words and thus learn how language works (Maclean, Bryant, and Bradley 1987).

Poetry and Literacy *(cont.)*

Phonics

The alliteration of *Goosie Goosie Gander* and the rhyming words of *Jack Sprat Could Eat No Fat* lay the groundwork for phonics instruction. Children can't *sound out* words if they don't hear the sounds. Decades of research have demonstrated that rhymes help children develop an ear for language. In one longitudinal study, researchers found a strong correlation between early knowledge of rhymes in children from ages three to six and success in reading and spelling over the next three years, even when accounting for differences in social background and I.Q. (Bryant, Bradley, Maclean, and Crossland 1989). Poetry and rhymes surround children with the sounds of language—sounds that must be applied in the letter-sound relationships of phonics instruction.

Vocabulary and Comprehension

Even a strong foundation in phonemic awareness and phonics is not enough. Students who can decode words but do not know their meanings usually struggle with comprehension, which is, of course, the ultimate goal of reading. Research has consistently shown a strong correlation between vocabulary and comprehension (Bromley 2007; Chall 1983; National Reading Panel 2000). Typical correlations between standardized measures of vocabulary and reading comprehension are in the .90 or higher range regardless of the measure used or the populations tested (Stahl 2003). Vocabulary development is just one more benefit of using poetry and rhymes with children. If you think it's too late for your third graders to read nursery rhymes, think again! Most nursery rhymes present opportunities to learn new vocabulary words that are relevant today but may not be familiar to many eight-year-olds (e.g., *platter* [Jack Sprat], *dainty* [Sing a Song of Sixpence], and *hickory* [Hickory Dickory Dock]).

Fluency

The repeated reading of poems and rhymes provides ample opportunities for students to develop reading fluency. Rasinski and Padak (2013) describe fluency as "a bridge that connects word decoding to comprehension . . . Fluency includes automatic word recognition, interpretive and prosodic reading, and appropriate expression and rate. Fluency is the ability to read expressively and meaningfully, as well as accurately and with appropriate speed" (252). Research into repeated readings indicates that reading a particular passage several times, which we suggest you do with the nursery rhymes and poems in this book, leads not only to fluency with that text but also transfers to new, unfamiliar text (Dowhower 1987, 1997; Rasinski et al. 1994; Samuels 1997; Stahl and Heubach 2005).

> *"Purposeful practice is essential for improvement and mastery of literacy skills. When given proper instruction, materials, and opportunities to practice and apply what they learn, all students can experience literacy success"* (Hackett 2013, 4).

Poetry and nursery rhymes send the all-important message that reading is fun. What children can resist the tickle in their mouths when they say *Fuzzy Wuzzy* or the onomatopoeia of *Baa Baa Black Sheep*? The natural rhythm and meter beg children to recite nursery rhymes over and over, increasing fluency skills more and more each time. Enjoy watching your students light up as they say each and every one of the rhymes in this book.

How to Use This Book

Implementing the Lessons

The following information explains the various activities in the lessons and how to implement them with students. Additional tips on how to implement the lessons can be found on pages 134–135.

Introducing the Rhyme

This section helps teachers introduce the poem to students. Use the steps listed below to introduce all of the poems in this book. Then, continue with the specific tasks mentioned in each lesson.

1. Copy the rhyme on a sheet of chart paper or on the board. (*optional*)

2. Read the rhyme to students.

3. Distribute copies of the rhyme to students.

4. Read the rhyme chorally several times to develop fluency.

5. Have students illustrate the rhyme and add it to their individual poetry notebooks. For more information about how to set up the poetry notebooks, see page 135.

Word Ladders

This activity allows students to build and examine words on an activity sheet. To begin, students are given a key word from the rhyme. In order to "climb the ladder," students must follow the teacher's clues and change the first word progressively, thus creating a new word at each step. Clues can require students to add, remove, change, or rearrange letters. The final word relates to the first word. For example, for the rhyme "Jack Sprat," students follow your instructions to progressively change the following words: *fat, cat, hat, hate, cake, lake, lame, lane, lean.*

Since this activity is teacher-led (the teacher reads the clues), it should be done as a whole-class activity, or you may wish to work with some students in a small group. Be sure to clarify any clues or word meanings that students may be unfamiliar with.

How to Use This Book *(cont.)*

Word Sorts

The *Word Sort* activity helps students explore relationships among words. Students are given a set of word cards related to the rhyme and work individually, in pairs, or in groups to sort the cards into two or more categories. Some will be *open* word sorts and some will be *closed* word sorts.

For open sorts, the categories are not predetermined. Students look for commonalities among the words and create their groups or categories accordingly. Then, they share their word sorts with classmates, explaining the groups they created. For example, given a set of picture cards (*skates*, *sandwich*, *doll*, *donut*) students could sort the cards by initial sounds (/s/ or /d/) or by function (toys and food). As long as they can justify their groups, the sorting is accepted. **Note:** You may find open word sorts are effective as pre-reading activities. The sorting allows students to become familiar with the words they will encounter in the rhymes. In addition, the sorting can help students predict what the text will be about. If used as a pre-reading activity, you will want to have them sort again after reading the rhyme in order to see if their categories change.

For closed word sorts, the categories are predetermined. The teacher instructs students to sort their words into specified categories. After the sorting, students discuss the words and why they were placed in the given categories. **Note**: For each closed word sort, we suggest categories for sorting the words. You can also come up with other categories for your students to use.

Rhyming Riddles

Each lesson includes a *Rhyming Riddles* activity. Students are instructed to use words in a word bank to answer riddles related to a key word or phrase from the rhyme. Students may be able to do this independently, or it can be conducted as a large group activity. Have students say as many rhyming words as they can to partners before implementing the activity sheets so that students know which rhyming sounds they are focusing on. You may wish to have them use the *My Rhyming Words* template (page 136) to write all of the rhyming words they brainstorm.

How to Use This Book (cont.)

Writing Connections

Each lesson includes a *Writing Connection* activity that relates to the rhyme in some way. The activities vary from students writing their own poems, to writing letters to characters in the rhymes, to making lists. We suggest that you use these lessons to generate enjoyment of writing rather than to teach grammar and spelling. **Note**: Have writing paper available for the *Writing Connection* in all lessons.

Reader's Theater

Each lesson includes a *Reader's Theater* script that focuses on the rhyme, where students are assigned parts of a script to read aloud. Oral language fluency is an important precursor to oral reading fluency. Fluent speakers actually help their listeners make sense of words and ideas by speaking at an appropriate pace, using meaningful phrases, and embedding expression and pauses into their speech—essentially the same skills needed for fluent reading (Rasinski and Padak 2013).

Have students rehearse the poem several times by themselves or in small groups to enhance listening and speaking skills and improve students' confidence. Arrange for various ways that students can then perform the poem as well as the accompanying script. Students can perform for classmates, another class, parents, the school principal, other teachers, or even record their reading for later performance. **Note**: There are not enough parts for every student in your class. Be sure to look over the amount of parts before assigning them to students.

All of the scripts provide opportunities for repeated reading, the benefits of which we discussed above. Rasinski and Padak (2013) call it "deep reading" (5) and suggest the following routine: "I'll read it to you. You read it with me. Now you read it alone" (66). The problem teachers sometimes face with repeated reading, particularly with older students, is motivating students to read a text multiple times. As one solution to that dilemma, each lesson has a suggestion for tying the repeated reading to a performance. Students should not be required to memorize the text for the performance but simply be prepared to read it aloud with confidence and with good expression.

If you think it's too late for your third graders to read nursery rhymes, think again! To make sure you're convinced, we've included a subtle humor into the reader's theater scripts, which will challenge your third graders to think at high levels about the rhymes (all the while laughing!) as they address the language arts standards.

Jack Sprat

Standards

◉ Refer to parts of stories, drama, and poems when writing or speaking about a text, using terms such as chapter, scene, and stanza; describe how each successive part builds on earlier sections.

◉ Use text features and search tools to locate information relevant to a given topic efficiently.

◉ Distinguish their own point of view from that of the narrator or those of the characters.

◉ See Appendix C for additional standards.

Materials

◉ *Jack Sprat* (page 11)

◉ *Jack Sprat Word Ladder* (page 12)

◉ *Jack Sprat Closed Word Sort* (page 13)

◉ *Jack Sprat Rhyming Riddles* (page 14)

◉ *Jack Sprat Reader's Theater* (pages 15–16)

Procedures

Introducing the Rhyme

1. Recite the rhyme to students. Tell students to close their eyes and make mental images of the rhyme as you read it to them.

2. Have students open their eyes and share their images. Guide the discussion as necessary with questions such as the following:

    ◉ What do you think Jack and his wife are eating?

    ◉ Name physical characteristics that describe Jack and his wife. How do you know they look like that?

    ◉ Do you think there are leftovers for dinner at their house?

3. Distribute the *Jack Sprat* rhyme (page 11) to students.

4. Read the rhyme chorally several times to develop fluency.

5. Allow students to illustrate the rhyme and add it to their individual poetry notebooks.

6. Have students add the title to their notebooks' tables of contents.

Word Ladder

1. Distribute *Jack Sprat Word Ladder* (page 12) to students.

2. Tell them to follow your clues to make a word ladder from *fat* to *lean*. Say the following:

    ◉ start at the bottom of the ladder—Jack Sprat couldn't eat this. (*fat*)

    ◉ change the beginning letter—an animal that chases mice (*cat*)

    ◉ change the beginning letter—something to wear on your head (*hat*)

    ◉ add one letter—a strong dislike (*hate*)

    ◉ change two letters—a birthday dessert (*cake*)

    ◉ change one letter—a body of water (*lake*)

    ◉ change one letter—to have a leg that won't move (*lame*)

    ◉ change one letter—a long dirt road (*lane*)

    ◉ rearrange the letters—Jack Sprat's wife couldn't eat this. (*lean*)

3. Help students make a meaningful connection between the poem and the first and last rungs of the ladder.

Jack Sprat *(cont.)*

Closed Word Sort

1. Distribute sets of the *Jack Sprat Closed Word Sort* cards (page 13) to individual students, pairs of students, or groups of students.

2. Ask students to sort the words according to the number of syllables in each word.

3. Follow the sorting with a discussion of word meanings and rules for syllabication.

4. Relate the words to the rhyme.

Rhyming Riddles

1. Have students think of as many words that rhyme with *meat* as they can. Have them tell their words to partners.

2. Distribute *Jack Sprat Rhyming Riddles* (page 14) to students and make connections between the words students come up with in Step 1 with the words in the Word Bank.

3. Instruct students to use the words from the Word Bank to complete the riddles. Students can also create their own riddles for the words from the Word Bank or from the list of words they came up with in Step 1.

4. Have students illustrate one of the rhyming riddles on the backs of their papers.

Writing Connection

1. Divide the class into seven teams.

2. Assign each team a day of the week.

3. Have each team develop a healthy menu for Jack and one for his wife for the assigned day. Include breakfast, lunch, dinner, and a bedtime snack.

4. Post the menus for other teams to browse during free reading time.

Reader's Theater

1. Distribute the *Jack Sprat Reader's Theater* script (pages 15–16) to students.

2. Allow students to read the script independently.

3. Discuss the script.

4. Assign parts for five readers.

5. Allow several rehearsals to develop fluency.

6. Perform the reader's theater for the class, another class, or for a special school event.

Jack Sprat

Traditional Rhyme

Jack Sprat could eat no fat

His wife could eat no lean.

And so between them both

They licked the platter clean.

Name: _____ Date: _____

Jack Sprat

Word Ladder

Directions: Listen to the clues. Then, write the words on the rungs below as you climb the ladder.

9.

8.

7.

6.

5.

4.

3.

2.

1.

Jack Sprat

Closed Word Sort

Directions: Cut apart the cards. Then, sort the words according to the number of syllables in each word.

fat	lean	vinegar
foods	healthy	vegetables
sandwiches	salad	fruit
fries	hamburgers	eat
cheese	peanut	licked
baloney	wife	ranch
Sprat	platters	clean
dressing	macaroni	Jack
butter	milk	banana

Name: _____ Date: _____

Jack Sprat

Rhyming Riddles

. . . .

Directions: Use words from the Word Bank to complete the riddles below.
Note: You will not use all of the words.

Word Bank

meat	cheat	beat
treat	feet	seat
wheat	heat	beet

1. eat something on Halloween

   eat a _____

2. eat a steak

   eat some _____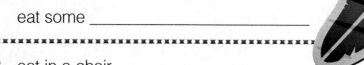

3. eat in a chair

   eat in your _____

4. eat when it's hot outside

   eat in the _____

5. eat grain

   eat _____

6. eat with drums playing

   eat to the _____

Jack Sprat

Reader's Theater

All: Jack Sprat

Reader 1: Here's an interesting rhyme:

Jack Sprat could eat no fat
His wife could eat no lean.
And so between them both
They licked the platter clean.

Reader 2: I've heard of people who can't eat fat, but I've never heard of a person who can't eat anything lean.

Reader 3: Me neither.

Reader 4: I eat pretty healthy foods. I don't think I get a lot of fat.

Reader 5: What are some of the foods you like to eat?

Reader 4: I like hamburgers, hot dogs, and French fries.

Reader 5: Those are all full of fat.

Reader 4: Okay. How about macaroni and cheese?
I love macaroni and cheese.

Reader 5: It's also full of fat.

Reader 4: Sometimes I like to eat sandwiches.

Reader 5: What kind?

Reader 4: Peanut butter or baloney sandwiches are my favorites.

Reader 5: Peanut butter and baloney both have fat in them, too.

Reader 3: How about a big dish of ice cream?

Reader 5: Ice cream is full of fat.

Reader 2: Jack Sprat must have been starving.

Jack Sprat

Reader's Theater *(cont.)*

Reader 3: What do you think he ate?

Reader 1: He probably ate lots of salad.

Reader 5: That wouldn't have fat in it, unless you add dressing.

Reader 3: The dressing is what makes salad so good.

Reader 1: He could add some vinegar. That doesn't have any fat in it.

Reader 3: Yes, but it certainly isn't as good as a salad covered in ranch dressing.

Reader 1: I think Jack Sprat ate lots of vegetables and fruit.

Reader 2: Don't those have any fat in them?

Reader 5: I don't think so, unless you add butter.

Reader 3: I would not like to be Jack Sprat.

Reader 2: Would you like to be like his wife?

Reader 4: Did she get to eat ice cream?

Reader 2: Of course.

Reader 4: Did she get to eat hot dogs, hamburgers, and French fries?

Reader 2: I'm sure she did.

Reader 4: Then, yes, I'd like to be like his wife.

Reader 5: Remember that his wife couldn't eat any lean foods. That means she couldn't eat fruit or vegetables. Could you give up fruit and vegetables?

Reader 4: I guess that would be okay with me.

Reader 2: I don't think Mrs. Sprat was very healthy.

Reader 3: I don't think Jack Sprat was very happy.

Reader 4: You're probably both right.

Going to St. Ives

Standards

◉ Ask and answer questions to demonstrate understanding of a text, referring explicitly to the text as the basis for the answers.

◉ Write opinion pieces on topics or texts, supporting a point of view with reasons. Provide reasons that support the opinion.

◉ See Appendix C for additional standards.

Materials

◉ *Going to St. Ives* (page 19)

◉ *Going to St. Ives Word Ladder* (page 20)

◉ *Going to St. Ives Open Word Sort* (page 21)

◉ *Going to St. Ives Rhyming Riddles* (page 22)

◉ *Going to St. Ives Reader's Theater* (pages 23–25)

Procedures

Introducing the Rhyme

1. Read the rhyme aloud to students.

2. Distribute the *Going to St. Ives* rhyme (page 19) to students.

3. Read the rhyme chorally several times to develop fluency.

4. Discuss possible answers to the St. Ives riddle: *How many were going to St. Ives?* Some answers may include:

   ◉ The rhyme states, *When I was going to St. Ives….* It does not say the man, wives, kits, and cats were going to St. Ives, so the answer would be *one* person going to St. Ives.

   ◉ Students can mathematically calculate how many were going if, indeed, the man, wives, kits, and cats were also traveling to St. Ives.

   ◉ If one considers that the cats and kits are in sacks, then one would only count the people because the kits and cats are "being taken," not "going."

   ◉ The final two lines state, *Kits, cats, sacks, wives; How many were going to St. Ives?* This excludes the man and the narrator from the total.

5. Allow students to illustrate the rhyme and add it to their individual poetry notebooks.

6. Have students add the title to their notebooks' tables of contents.

Word Ladder

1. Distribute *Going to St. Ives Word Ladder* (page 20) to students.

2. Tell them to follow your clues to make a word ladder from *wife* to *kit.* Say the following:

   ◉ start at the bottom of the ladder—singular noun for what the man in the rhyme had seven of (*wife*)

   ◉ change one letter—If something is living, it has this. (*life*)

   ◉ change one letter—to raise something up (*lift*)

   ◉ change one letter—to separate and retain the coarse parts of flour with a sieve (*sift*)

   ◉ remove one letter—You train your dog to do this. (*sit*)

   ◉ change one letter—You did this to an apple. (*bit*)

   ◉ add one letter—what a mean dog might do (*bite*)

   ◉ change one letter—an object that flies on a string (*kite*)

   ◉ remove one letter—what each cat in the rhyme had seven of (*kit*)

3. Help students make a meaningful connection between the poem and the first and last rungs of the ladder.

Going to St. Ives *(cont.)*

Open Word Sort

1. Distribute sets of the *Going to St. Ives Open Word Sort* cards (page 21) to individual students, pairs of students, or groups of students.

2. This is an open word sort. Have students read the words and decide how they can be sorted.

3. Follow the sorting with a discussion of word meanings and the different ways word groups were created.

4. Relate the words to the rhyme.

Rhyming Riddles

1. Have students think of as many words that rhyme with *Ives* as they can. Have them tell their words to partners.

2. Distribute *Going to St. Ives Rhyming Riddles* (page 22) to students and make connections between the words students come up with in Step 1 with the words in the Word Bank.

3. Instruct students to use the words from the Word Bank to complete the riddles. Students can also create their own riddles for the words from the Word Bank or from the list of words they came up with in Step 1.

4. Have students illustrate one of the rhyming riddles on the backs of their papers.

Writing Connection

1. Have students think back to the discussion about the riddle from the *Introducing the Rhyme* section.

2. Ask students to write their conclusions about how many were going to St. Ives, including their reasons for the choices they made.

3. Allow volunteers to read their compositions to the class.

Reader's Theater

1. Distribute the *Going to St. Ives Reader's Theater* script (pages 23–25) to students.

2. Allow students to read the script independently.

3. Discuss the script.

4. Assign parts for seven readers.

5. Allow several rehearsals to develop fluency.

6. Perform the reader's theater for the class, another class, or for a special school event.

Going to St. Ives

Traditional Rhyme

As I was going to St. Ives

I met a man with seven wives.

Every wife had seven sacks.

Every sack had seven cats.

Every cat had seven kits.

Kits, cats, sacks, wives.

How many were going to St. Ives?

Name: _____ Date: _____

Going to St. Ives

Word Ladder

Directions: Listen to the clues. Then, write the words on the rungs below as you climb the ladder.

9.

8.

7.

6.

5.

4.

3.

2.

1.

Going to St. Ives

Open Word Sort

Directions: Cut apart the cards. Then, sort them into groups that you choose. Be ready to explain your groups.

Ives	lives
kits	man
sack	wife
caves	cakes
kite	kit
cat	wives
cats	kittens
known	cake
lakes	lake

Name: _____ Date: _____

Going to St. Ives

Rhyming Riddles

Directions: Use words from the Word Bank to complete the riddles below.
Note: You will not use all of the words.

Word Bank

lives	drive	survive
five	dive	strive
thrive	hives	knives

1. wives who operate cars

   wives who _____

2. wives chopping vegetables

   wives with _____

3. wives jumping in the pool

   wives who _____

4. wives who stepped on bees' nests

   wives stepping on _____

5. wives who try really hard

   wives who _____

6. wives who weren't hurt in an accident

   wives who _____

Going to St. Ives
Reader's Theater

All: Going to St. Ives

Reader 1: As I was going to St. Ives
I met a man with seven wives

Reader 2: Seven wives! Isn't that against the law?

Reader 3: I'm pretty sure it is.

Reader 4: Then, what was he doing with seven wives?

Reader 1: I don't know. I didn't write the rhyme. I'm just trying to recite it.

Reader 2: Okay. Go ahead. This should be interesting.

Reader 1: As I was going to St. Ives
I met a man with seven wives.
Every wife had seven sacks.

Reader 5: What was in them?

Reader 1: What?

Reader 5: What was in the seven sacks? Was it food? I hope it was food.

Reader 1: Why?

Reader 5: It would cost a lot of money to take seven wives to a restaurant. Packing a lunch is a better idea.

Going to St. Ives

Reader's Theater *(cont.)*

Reader 1: Whatever was in the sacks is in the rhyme. Let me finish it.

As I was going to St. Ives
I met a man with seven wives.
Every wife had seven sacks.
Every sack had seven cats.
Every cat had seven kits.

Reader 6: Wow! Do you realize how many cats and kittens those wives were carrying?

Reader 7: It sounds like a lot.

Reader 6: Let me see. If just one sack had 7 cats in it and each of those cats had 7 kittens with them, it would be 7 times 7, plus the mother cats. That's 56 cats in one sack! And if each wife was carrying 7 sacks, that would be 7 times 56. Let's see; 7 times 56. Oh my gosh! Each wife was carrying a total of 392 cats and kittens!

Reader 5: And don't forget there were 7 wives. So let's figure this out. 7 wives times 392 cats would be 2,744 cats!

Reader 3: Where did they get them all? Did they rob a pound?

Reader 1: I have no idea. I also have no idea how they carried them all.

Reader 2: And another thing, why were the cats and kittens in sacks?

Reader 4: They probably couldn't find a box big enough to put them all into.

Reader 5: What they really needed was a truck—a very BIG truck. Is that the end of the rhyme?

Going to St. Ives

Reader's Theater (cont.)

Reader 1: No. Here's the rest. I'll start at the beginning again.

As I was going to St. Ives
I met a man with seven wives.
Every wife had seven sacks.
Every sack had seven cats.
Every cat had seven kits.
Kits, cats, sacks, and wives.
How many were going to St. Ives?

Reader 5: Well, we already did the math on the cats. So if there were 2,744 cats and kittens and seven wives, and one husband, that would be 2,752 total who were going to St. Ives.

Reader 1: That's wrong.

Reader 5: What do you mean it's wrong?
Listen to the first line again.
As I was going to St. Ives.

Reader 5: Okay. I forgot one. That would be 2,410 then.

Reader 1: No. You're not listening. According to that first line, there was only one going to St. Ives.

Reader 3: You can't be sure of that.

Reader 1: What do you mean? The rhyme said, "As I was going to St. Ives." It didn't say all those others were going to St. Ives.

Reader 2: But it didn't say they weren't, either. The rhyme just said he met them as he was going to St. Ives. They could have been on their way to St. Ives, too.

Reader 3: Well if they were, I hope they have a big house there.

Reader 1: Why?

Reader 3: They're going to need one with all of those cats.

Sing a Song of Sixpence

Standards

◎ Refer to parts of stories, dramas, and poems when writing or speaking about a text, using terms such as chapter, scene, and stanza; describe how each successive part builds on earlier sections.

◎ Produce writing in which the development and organization are appropriate to task and purpose.

◎ See Appendix C for additional standards.

Materials

◎ *Sing a Song of Sixpence* (page 28)

◎ *Sing a Song of Sixpence Word Ladder* (page 29)

◎ *Sing a Song of Sixpence Open Word Sort* (page 30)

◎ *Sing a Song of Sixpence Rhyming Riddles* (page 31)

◎ *Sing a Song of Sixpence Reader's Theater* (pages 32–34)

Procedures

Introducing the Rhyme

1. Distribute the *Sing a Song of Sixpence* rhyme (page 28) to students.

2. Read (or sing) the rhyme to students.

3. Discuss the term *stanza* with students. After listening to the rhyme, ask students to help detect the rhythm and rhyme that make up the stanzas.

4. Divide the class into four groups, and assign each group a stanza to read.

5. Allow students to illustrate the rhyme and add it to their individual poetry notebooks.

6. Have students add the title to their notebooks' tables of contents.

Word Ladder

1. Distribute *Sing a Song of Sixpence Word Ladder* (page 29) to students.

2. Tell them to follow your clues to make a word ladder from *sing* to *song*. Say the following:

   ◎ start at the bottom of the ladder—When the pie was open, the birds began to do this. (*sing*)

   ◎ change one letter—what birds need to fly (*wing*)

   ◎ remove one letter—what the best team does (*win*)

   ◎ change the vowel—the past tense of Number 3 (*won*)

   ◎ add one letter and an apostrophe—contraction for will not (*won't*)

   ◎ change one letter—contraction for do not (*don't*)

   ◎ remove two letters and the apostrophe—opposite of don't (*do*)

   ◎ add two letters—You are finished. (*done*)

   ◎ change a letter—the sound of a door bell: ding-_____ (*dong*)

   ◎ change a letter—The birds sang a _____. (*song*)

3. Help students make a meaningful connection between the poem and the first and last rungs of the ladder.

Sing a Song of Sixpence (cont.)

Open Word Sort

1. Distribute sets of the *Sing a Song of Sixpence Open Word Sort* cards (page 30) to individual students, pairs of students, or groups of students.

2. Have students read the words and decide how they can be sorted.

3. Follow the sorting with a discussion of word meanings and the different ways word groups were created.

4. Relate the words to the rhyme.

Rhyming Riddles

1. Have students think of as many words that rhyme with *king* as they can. Have them tell their words to partners.

2. Distribute *Sing a Song of Sixpence Rhyming Riddles* (page 31) to students and make connections between the words students come up with in Step 1 with the words in the Word Bank.

3. Instruct students to use the words from the Word Bank to complete the riddles. Students can also create their own riddles for the words from the Word Bank or from the list of words they came up with in Step 1.

4. Have students illustrate one of the rhyming riddles on the backs of their papers.

Writing Connection

1. Have students assume the role of king or queen and write letters to the royal cook regarding the pie.

2. Post the letters around the room.

3. Allow students to move around the room in small groups, reading and commenting on the letters.

Reader's Theater

1. Distribute the *Sing a Song of Sixpence Reader's Theater* script (pages 32–34) to students.

2. Allow students to read the script independently.

3. Discuss the script.

4. Assign parts for five readers.

5. Allow several rehearsals to develop fluency.

6. Perform the reader's theater for the class, another class, or for a special school event.

Sing a Song of Sixpence

Traditional Rhyme

Sing a song of sixpence,
A pocket full of rye;
Four and twenty blackbirds
Baked in a pie.

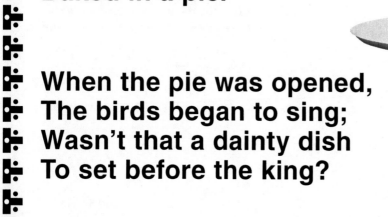

When the pie was opened,
The birds began to sing;
Wasn't that a dainty dish
To set before the king?

The king was in his counting-house
Counting out his money;
The queen was in the parlor
Eating bread and honey;

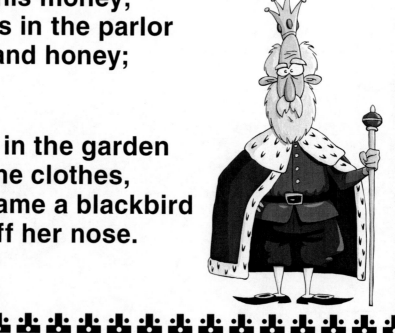

The maid was in the garden
Hanging out the clothes,
When along came a blackbird
And pecked off her nose.

Name: _____ Date: _____

Sing a Song of Sixpence

Word Ladder

· ·

Directions: Listen to the clues. Then, write the words on the rungs below as you climb the ladder.

10.

9.

8.

7.

6.

5.

4.

3.

2.

1.

Sing a Song of Sixpence

Open Word Sort

. . . .

Directions: Cut apart the cards. Then, sort them into groups that you choose.
Be ready to explain your groups.

sing	song	maid
rye	pocket	clothes
birds	coin	queen
wheat	grain	garden
bread	sixpence	known
pie	dish	honey
king	money	dainty

Name: _____   Date: _____

Sing a Song of Sixpence

Rhyming Riddles

Directions: Use words from the Word Bank to complete the riddles below.
Note: You will not use all of the words.

Word Bank

sting	fling	wings
bring	swing	spring
ring	sing	string

1. a king who flies

a king with _____

2. the king's favorite season

The king loves _____ .

3. A bee was angry with the king.

The king got a _____ .

4. The king likes the playground.

a king on a _____

5. a king who ties things

a king with _____

6. jewelry on a king's finger

a king wearing a _____

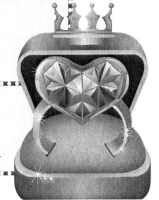

Sing a Song of Sixpence

Reader's Theater

All: Sing a Song of Sixpence

Reader 1: Sing a song of sixpence,
A pocket full of rye;

Reader 2: What is a *sixpence*?

Reader 1: I think it's an old English coin.

Reader 2: Okay. What is *rye*?

Reader 3: I think it's a kind of grain similar to wheat.
They use it to make rye bread.

Reader 2: So somebody made a rhyme about money and grain?

Reader 1: Not exactly. Let me read the rest of it:
Sing a song of sixpence,
A pocket full of rye;
Four and twenty blackbirds
Baked in a pie.

Reader 4: A blackbird pie?! Who would make a blackbird pie in the first
place, and who would want to eat something like that?

Reader 1: I'm not sure. It's a very old rhyme. Maybe
that's the kind of stuff they ate back then.

Reader 5: Is that the end of the rhyme?

Sing a Song of Sixpence

Reader's Theater *(cont.)*

Reader 1: No there's more:
When the pie was opened,
The birds began to sing;
Wasn't that a dainty dish
To set before the king?

Reader 4: The birds were alive?! I thought you said they were baked. How did they survive being baked? And why were they singing? They should have flown away right there and then.

Reader 1: I don't know. Maybe the oven wasn't hot and maybe they were singing because they were getting ready to fly away.

Readers 2–5: Fly, blackbirds, fly!

Reader 1: Here's the next stanza:
The king was in his counting-house
Counting out his money;
The queen was in the parlor
Eating bread and honey;

Reader 4: She was eating bread and honey because she didn't want anything to do with a pie with live blackbirds in it.

Reader 1: Can I finish?

Reader 3: Go ahead.

Sing a Song of Sixpence

Reader's Theater *(cont.)*

Reader 1: The maid was in the garden
Hanging out the clothes,
When along came a blackbird
And pecked off her nose.

Reader 4: That's more like it! The
blackbirds are on the attack.
They need to go after the
guy who put them in that
pie in the first place and
then go after the king.

All: Go, blackbirds, go!

Reader 2: Let's hope they all got away.

Reader 3: Let's hope the king tried apple pie and liked it better.

Pease Porridge Hot

Standards

- Refer to parts of stories, dramas, and poems when writing or speaking about a text, using terms such as chapter, scene, and stanza; describe how each successive part builds on earlier sections.

- Use glossaries or beginning dictionaries, both print and digital, to determine or clarify the precise meaning of key words and phrases.

- See Appendix C for additional standards.

Materials

- *Pease Porridge Hot* (page 37)

- *Pease Porridge Hot Word Ladder* (page 38)

- *Pease Porridge Hot Closed Word Sort* (page 39)

- *Pease Porridge Hot Rhyming Riddles* (page 40)

- *Pease Porridge Hot Reader's Theater* (pages 41–43)

Procedures

Introducing the Rhyme

1. Distribute the *Pease Porridge Hot* rhyme (page 37) to students.

2. Read the rhyme chorally.

3. Discuss the term *stanza* with students. After listening to the rhyme, ask students to help identify the stanzas in the rhyme.

4. Help students use an online dictionary to look up the definition of the word *pease* (an archaic word for *peas)*.

5. Divide students into pairs. Teach them a hand-clapping game to use with the rhyme. Any hand-clapping game you did as a child will work (e.g., Miss Mary Mack, Miss Lucy Had a Baby).

6. Allow students to illustrate the rhyme and add it to their individual poetry notebooks.

7. Have students add the title to their notebooks' tables of contents.

Word Ladder

1. Distribute *Pease Porridge Hot Word Ladder* (page 38) to students.

2. Tell them to follow your clues to make a word ladder from *hot* to *cold*. Say the following:

   - start at the bottom of the ladder—the temperature of pease porridge at the beginning of the rhyme (*hot*)

   - change one letter—something you can sleep on (*cot*)

   - change two letters—what soup comes in (*can*)

   - add one letter—a walking stick (*cane*)

   - change one letter—what you put ice cream in (*cone*)

   - change one letter—A dog likes this. (*bone*)

   - change last two letters—a word for very brave (*bold*)

   - change one letter—what you do with your clothes (*fold*)

   - change one letter—another temperature of pease porridge (*cold*)

3. Help students make a meaningful connection between the poem and the first and last rungs of the ladder.

Pease Porridge Hot *(cont.)*

Closed Word Sort

1. Distribute sets of the *Pease Porridge Hot Closed Word Sort* cards (page 39) to individual students, pairs of students, or groups of students.

2. Ask students to sort the words according to vowel sounds.

3. Follow the sorting with a discussion of word meanings and the vowel rules.

4. Relate the words to the rhyme.

Rhyming Riddles

1. Have students think of as many words that rhyme with *pease* as they can. Have them tell their words to partners.

2. Distribute *Pease Porridge Hot Rhyming Riddles* (page 40) to students and make connections between the words students come up with in Step 1 with the words in the Word Bank.

3. Instruct students to use the words from the Word Bank to complete the riddles. Students can also create their own riddles for the words from the Word Bank or from the list of words they came up with in Step 1.

4. Have students illustrate one of the rhyming riddles on the backs of their papers.

Writing Connection

1. Ask students to count the syllables in each line as they recite the rhyme.

2. Write the pattern on the board:

   4 syllables

   4 syllables

   6 syllables

   3 syllables

3. Have students write their own rhymes following the pattern they discovered in *Pease Porridge Hot*. Students can write as many stanzas as they wish. The following is an example:

   Do what you want.

   Do what you like.

   I'm having fun today

   on my bike.

4. Invite another class or two to join you for a poetry slam. A poetry slam is a competition that puts dual emphasis on writing and performing poetry. The audience votes for the best performance.

Reader's Theater

1. Distribute the *Pease Porridge Hot Reader's Theater* script (pages 41–43) to students.

2. Allow students to read the script independently.

3. Discuss the script.

4. Assign parts for six readers.

5. Allow several rehearsals to develop fluency.

6. Perform the reader's theater for the class, another class, or for a special school event.

Pease Porridge Hot

Traditional Rhyme

Pease porridge hot,

Pease porridge cold,

Pease porridge in the pot

Nine days old.

Some like it hot,

Some like it cold,

Some like it in the pot

Nine days old.

Name: _____ Date: _____

Pease Porridge Hot

Word Ladder

· ·

Directions: Listen to the clues. Then, write the words on the rungs below as you climb the ladder.

9.

8.

7.

6.

5.

4.

3.

2.

1.

Pease Porridge Hot

Closed Word Sort

Directions: Cut apart the cards. Then, sort the words according to their vowel sounds.

hot	cold
old	oatmeal
peaches	eats
pan	sick
slow	quick
lunch	pease
pot	nine
days	like

Name: _____ Date: _____

Pease Porridge Hot

Rhyming Riddles

Directions: Use words from the Word Bank to complete the riddles below.
Note: You will not use all of the words.

Word Bank

disease	trees	squeeze
ease	please	breeze
sneeze	tease	leaves

1. peas that say, "Achoo!"

   peas that _____

2. peas that hug too tight

   peas that _____

3. peas raking in the fall

   peas raking _____

4. peas building nests

   peas in _____

5. peas flying in the wind

   peas in the _____

6. peas that are polite

   peas saying _____

Pease Porridge Hot

Reader's Theater

All: Pease Porridge Hot

Reader 1: This one's called *Pease Porridge Hot.*

Reader 2: What is pease porridge?

Reader 1: Well, I think that porridge is like oatmeal.

Reader 3: And pease?

Reader 1: I guess that means peas.

Reader 4: Peas in oatmeal?! That's disgusting! I've tasted blueberries in oatmeal and peaches in oatmeal, but I would never eat oatmeal with peas in it.

Reader 1: Me neither, but that is the title of the rhyme.

Reader 2: Go ahead and read it. I can hardly wait.

Reader 1: Okay. Here goes.

Pease porridge hot,
Pease porridge cold,

Reader 5: Cold oatmeal?! Who ever heard of cold oatmeal? I wouldn't eat regular oatmeal cold and I certainly wouldn't eat cold oatmeal with peas in it. Who eats this kind of stuff?

Reader 6: Maybe someone who's really hungry would eat it.

Reader 2: I would have to be starving to eat cold oatmeal with peas in it.

Pease Porridge Hot

Reader's Theater (cont.)

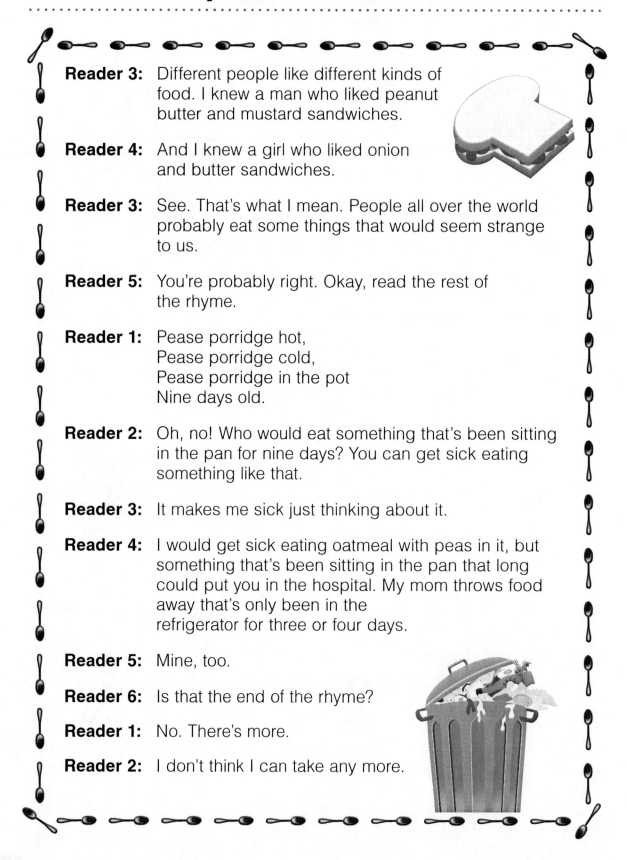

Reader 3: Different people like different kinds of food. I knew a man who liked peanut butter and mustard sandwiches.

Reader 4: And I knew a girl who liked onion and butter sandwiches.

Reader 3: See. That's what I mean. People all over the world probably eat some things that would seem strange to us.

Reader 5: You're probably right. Okay, read the rest of the rhyme.

Reader 1: Pease porridge hot,
Pease porridge cold,
Pease porridge in the pot
Nine days old.

Reader 2: Oh, no! Who would eat something that's been sitting in the pan for nine days? You can get sick eating something like that.

Reader 3: It makes me sick just thinking about it.

Reader 4: I would get sick eating oatmeal with peas in it, but something that's been sitting in the pan that long could put you in the hospital. My mom throws food away that's only been in the refrigerator for three or four days.

Reader 5: Mine, too.

Reader 6: Is that the end of the rhyme?

Reader 1: No. There's more.

Reader 2: I don't think I can take any more.

Pease Porridge Hot

Reader's Theater *(cont.)*

Reader 1: Here's the second stanza.

Some like it hot,
Some like it cold,
Some like it in the pot
Nine days old.

Reader 5: I'd like to add a third verse.

Reader 1: Okay. What is it?

Reader 5: Some eat it slow.
Some eat it quick.
If it's been in the pot that long,
It's sure to make you sick.

Reader 4: Good job.

Reader 5: Thanks.

Reader 3: I may never be able to look at oatmeal again without thinking about peas in it.

Reader 4: And I won't be able to eat peas without thinking about them being mixed with oatmeal.

Reader 6: Is it almost lunchtime?

Reader 2: Why?

Reader 6: I need to taste something good to get the thought of oatmeal with peas out of my head.

Reader 2: Me, too.

Readers 2–6: I hope they don't serve peas.

Reader 1: Or oatmeal cookies.

Hickory Dickory Dock

Standards

◎ Read with sufficient accuracy and fluency to support comprehension.

◎ Acquire and use accurately grade-appropriate conversational, general academic, and domain-specific words and phrases, including those that signal spatial and temporal relationships.

◎ See Appendix C for additional standards.

Materials

◎ *Hickory Dickory Dock* (page 46)

◎ *Hickory Dickory Dock Word Ladder* (page 47)

◎ *Hickory Dickory Dock Open Word Sort* (page 48)

◎ *Hickory Dickory Dock Rhyming Riddles* (page 49)

◎ *Hickory Dickory Dock Reader's Theater* (pages 50–52)

Procedures

Introducing the Rhyme

1. Distribute the *Hickory Dickory Dock* rhyme (page 46) to students.

2. Divide the class into nine groups.

3. Since this is one of the more common nursery rhymes, all or most of your students may be able to recite it without the text. In order to encourage students to attend to print, divide the class and ask them to mark their parts. Then, instruct them to follow the print so that the reading is fluent, as if one voice were reading the entire rhyme.

Group 1:	Hickory
Group 2:	Dickory
Group 3:	Dock
Group 4:	The mouse ran up the clock.
Group 5:	The clock struck one
Group 6:	And down he run
Group 7:	Hickory
Group 8:	Dickory
Group 9:	Dock

4. Allow students to illustrate the rhyme and add it to their individual poetry notebooks.

5. Have students add the title to their notebooks' tables of contents.

Word Ladder

1. Distribute *Hickory Dickory Dock Word Ladder* (page 47) to students.

2. Tell them to follow your clues to make a word ladder from *dock* to *hickory*. Say the following:

   ◎ start at the bottom of the ladder—the last word of this rhyme (*dock*)

   ◎ change one letter—something you wear on your foot (*sock*)

   ◎ change the vowel—another word for ill (*sick*)

   ◎ change one letter—half of the sound a clock makes (*tick*)

   ◎ change one letter—what you do with a lollipop (*lick*)

   ◎ add a letter—the sound made when you snap your fingers (*click*)

   ◎ change the beginning blend—a small hen (*chick*)

   ◎ remove two letters—part of a hiccup (*hic*)

   ◎ add four letters—the first word of this rhyme (*hickory*)

3. Help students make a meaningful connection between the poem and the first and last rungs of the ladder.

Hickory Dickory Dock (cont.)

Open Word Sort

1. Distribute sets of the *Hickory Dickory Dock Open Word Sort* cards (page 48) to individual students, pairs of students, or groups of students.

2. Have students read the words and decide how they can be sorted.

3. Follow the sorting with a discussion of word meanings and the different ways word groups were created.

4. Relate the words to the rhyme.

Rhyming Riddles

1. Have students think of as many words that rhyme with *dock* as they can. Have them tell their words to partners.

2. Distribute *Hickory Dickory Dock Rhyming Riddles* (page 49) to students and make connections between the words students come up with in Step 1 with the words in the Word Bank.

3. Instruct students to use the words from the Word Bank to complete the riddles. Students can also create their own riddles for the words from the Word Bank or from the list of words they came up with in Step 1.

4. Have students illustrate one of the rhyming riddles on the backs of their papers.

Writing Connection

1. Have students write copy changes of *Hickory Dickory Dock* using the AA, BB, A changing pattern below. Copy change is a writing activity where the writer borrows the structure of another text and uses it as a skeleton for his or her own piece.

Hickory Dickory _____ (A)

_____ (A)

_____ (B)

_____ (B)

Hickory Dickory _____ (A)

Example
Hickory Dickory Dack
I think I'm getting the knack
For writing rhymes
That sound just fine
Hickory Dickory Dack

2. Have students share their rhymes with the class.

Reader's Theater

1. Distribute the *Hickory Dickory Dock Reader's Theater* script (pages 50–52) to students.

2. Allow students to read the script independently.

3. Discuss the script.

4. Assign parts for five readers.

5. Allow several rehearsals to develop fluency.

6. Perform the reader's theater for the class, another class, or for a special school event.

Hickory Dickory Dock

Traditional Rhyme

Hickory, dickory, dock,

The mouse ran up the clock.

The clock struck one

And down he run

Hickory, dickory, dock.

Name: _____ Date: _____

Hickory Dickory Dock
Word Ladder

Directions: Listen to the clues. Then, write the words on the rungs below as you climb the ladder.

9.

8.

7.

6.

5.

4.

3.

2.

1.

Hickory Dickory Dock

Open Word Sort

Directions: Cut apart the cards. Then, sort them into groups or categories that you choose. Be ready to explain your groups.

mouse	clock	down
grandfather	alarm	strike
mice	hickory	pendulum
elm	dock	up
chimes	bell	boat
rings	buzz	ran
one	three	battery
oak	mice	wristwatch

Name: _____ Date: _____

Hickory Dickory Dock

Rhyming Riddles

Directions: Use words from the Word Bank to complete the riddles below.
Note: You will not use all of the words.

Word Bank

socks	stock	dock
knock	lock	flock
shock	rock	block

1. clocks with covered feet

clocks wearing _____

2. clocks with a key

clocks that _____

3. clocks that love loud music

clocks that _____

4. clocks on the pier

clocks on the _____

5. clocks that touched an electric wire

clocks that got a _____

6. clocks pounding on the door

clocks that _____

Hickory Dickory Dock

Reader's Theater

All: Hickory Dickory Dock

Reader 1: Hickory, Dickory, Dock
The mouse ran up the clock . . .

Reader 2: Why?

Reader 1: Why what?

Reader 2: Why did the mouse run up
the clock?

Reader 1: I don't know. Maybe he didn't
have anything better to do.

Reader 3: Was it an alarm clock?

Reader 1: I don't know.

Reader 4: If it was an alarm clock, he wouldn't
have to run up it. He could just jump.

Reader 1: I don't think it was an alarm clock. I think it was a
grandfather clock.

Reader 5: What's a grandfather clock?

Reader 2: It's one of those old-fashioned clocks that sits on
the floor. It's made out of wood with the clock part
at the top and the big pendulum on the bottom.

Reader 3: What's a pendulum?

Hickory Dickory Dock

Reader's Theater (cont.)

Reader 2: A pendulum is a big metal piece that swings back and forth. The swinging action keeps the clock working.

Reader 4: Why can't you just put a battery in it to keep it working?

Reader 2: Because when grandfather clocks were first made many years ago, batteries had not been invented.

Reader 3: So you think the mouse climbed up a grandfather clock?

Reader 1: Yes. Let me start the rhyme again.

Readers 2–5: Okay.

Reader 1: Hickory, dickory, dock
The mouse ran up the clock.
The clock struck one . . .

Reader 2: Wait a minute. I thought you said there was only one mouse.

Reader 1: There was.

Reader 2: But you just said the clock struck one. Where's the other one?

Reader 1: I meant the clock struck one o'clock.

Hickory Dickory Dock

Reader's Theater *(cont.)*

Reader 3: Now I'm really confused. How can a clock strike something?

Reader 1: Every time a grandfather clock reaches a new hour, a gong inside of it hits a bell. They call that hit a strike. If it's one o'clock, it strikes once, if it's two o'clock it strikes twice and so on. So when I said, "the clock struck one," it means it was one o'clock.

Reader 3: Oh. Now I understand. Okay, read the rest of the rhyme.

Reader 1: I'll start at the beginning:
Hickory, dickory, dock,
The mouse ran up the clock.
The clock struck one
And down he run
Hickory, dickory, dock.

Reader 4: Is that it?

Reader 1: That's it.

Readers 2–5: Nice rhyme.

Reader 1: Thanks.

Little Miss Muffet

Standards

◎ Use glossaries or beginning dictionaries, both print and digital, to determine or clarify the precise meaning of key words and phrases.

◎ Use dialogue and descriptions of actions, thoughts, and feelings to develop experiences and events to show the response of characters to situations.

◎ See Appendix C for additional standards.

Materials

◎ *Little Miss Muffet* (page 55)

◎ *Little Miss Muffet Word Ladder* (page 56)

◎ *Little Miss Muffet Open Word Sort* (page 57)

◎ *Little Miss Muffet Rhyming Riddles* (page 58)

◎ *Little Miss Muffet Reader's Theater* (pages 59–61)

Procedures

Introducing the Rhyme

1. Distribute the *Little Miss Muffet* rhyme (page 55) to students.

2. Read the rhyme chorally several times to develop fluency.

3. Guide students in using a dictionary or online resource to define the words *tuffet*, *curds*, and *whey*.

4. Allow students to illustrate the rhyme and add it to their individual poetry notebooks.

5. Have students add the title to their notebooks' tables of contents.

Word Ladder

1. Distribute *Little Miss Muffet Word Ladder* (page 56) to students.

2. Tell them to follow your clues to make a word ladder from *Muffet* to *Miss*. Say the following:

   ◎ start at the bottom of the ladder—the little girl's last name (*Muffet*)

   ◎ change two letters at the end—a small, cup-shaped bread (*muffin*)

   ◎ change two consonants and one vowel—meat from lamb (*mutton*)

   ◎ change one letter—it holds your shirt together (*button*)

   ◎ take away three letters—2,000 pounds (*ton*)

   ◎ change one letter—a number (*ten*)

   ◎ add three letters—something you wear on your hands (*mitten*)

   ◎ remove two letters—another name for a baseball glove (*mitt*)

   ◎ change two letters—the second word in the title of the rhyme (*Miss*)

3. Help students make a meaningful connection between the poem and the first and last rungs of the ladder.

Little Miss Muffet *(cont.)*

Open Word Sort

1. Distribute sets of the *Little Miss Muffet Open Word Sort* cards (page 57) to individual students, pairs of students, or groups of students.

2. Have students read the words and decide how they can be sorted.

3. Follow the sorting with a discussion of word meanings and the different ways word groups were created.

4. Relate the words to the rhyme.

Rhyming Riddles

1. Have students think of as many words that rhyme with *spider* as they can. Have them tell their words to partners.

2. Distribute *Little Miss Muffet Rhyming Riddles* (page 58) to students and make connections between the words students come up with in Step 1 and the words in the Word Bank.

3. Instruct students to use the words from the Word Bank to complete the riddles. Students can also create their own riddles for the words from the Word Bank or from the list of words they came up with in Step 1.

4. Have students illustrate one of the rhyming riddles on the backs of their papers.

Writing Connection

1. Have students write a dialogue between Miss Muffet and the spider.

2. Have students share their writing with the class.

Reader's Theater

1. Distribute the *Little Miss Muffet Reader's Theater* script (pages 59–61) to students.

2. Allow students to read the script independently.

3. Discuss the script.

4. Assign parts for five readers.

5. Allow several rehearsals to develop fluency.

6. Perform the reader's theater for the class, another class, or for a special school event.

Little Miss Muffet

Traditional Rhyme

Little Miss Muffet

Sat on a tuffet

Eating her curds and whey.

Along came a spider

And sat down beside her

And frightened Miss Muffet away.

Name: _____ Date: _____

Little Miss Muffet

Word Ladder

· ·

Directions: Listen to the clues. Then, write the words on the rungs below as you climb the ladder.

9.

8.

7.

6.

5.

4.

3.

2.

1.

Little Miss Muffet

Open Word Sort

Directions: Cut apart the cards. Then, sort them into groups that you choose. Be ready to explain your groups.

spider	arachnid	tuffet
scorpion	eating	seat
daddy longlegs	running	patch of grass
bites	crawling	cookies
venom	spinning	milk
webs	victim	stool
curds	whey	Miss Muffet
prey	predator	cheese
cottage cheese	insect	chair

Name: _____ Date: _____

Little Miss Muffet

Rhyming Riddles

Directions: Use words from the Word Bank to complete the riddles below.
Note: You will not use all of the words.

Word Bank

wider	fighters	tighter
dividers	firefighter	lighter
gliders	cider	highlighter

1. spiders that drink apple juice

   spiders drinking _____

2. spiders that hit you

   spiders that are _____

3. spiders doing division problems

   spiders that are _____

4. spiders that are not very dark

   spiders that are _____

5. spiders in little airplanes

   spiders in _____

6. spiders that squeeze you

   spiders holding _____

Little Miss Muffet

Reader's Theater

All:　　　Little Miss Muffet

Reader 1:　I'm going to read a rhyme.

Reader 2:　Oh good. I love rhymes.

Reader 1:　Little Miss Muffet
　　　　　　Sat on a tuffet

Reader 2:　A what?

Reader 1:　A tuffet.

Reader 3:　What's a *tuffet*? I've never heard of a tuffet.

Reader 1:　I don't know what it is. Maybe it's some kind of chair.

Reader 4:　Well, why don't they just say she sat on a chair?

Reader 5:　Because it wouldn't rhyme with *Muffet.*

Reader 4:　Yes, but at least we would know what she sat on.

Reader 1:　Let's just pretend a tuffet is a chair.

Reader 2:　What if it's not a chair? What if a tuffet is a big bug?

Reader 3:　She wouldn't sit on a bug.

Reader 4:　She might if she didn't see it.

Reader 1:　We'll look up the word *tuffet* later in the dictionary. I just
　　　　　　want to finish reading the rhyme. Okay?

Little Miss Muffet

Reader's Theater (cont.)

Readers 2-5: Go ahead.

Reader 1: Little Miss Muffet
Sat on a tuffet,
Eating her curds and whey

Reader 5: What are *curds* and *whey*?

Reader 1: I'm not sure.

Reader 4: We don't know what she was
sitting on, now we don't know what she was eating.

Reader 1: Does it matter?

Reader 4: Yes, it matters. I'm trying to picture this person in my
mind as you read, but I can't do that without the facts.

Reader 1: Just pretend curds and whey are milk and cookies.

Reader 2: What if it's really spinach and beets? I hate spinach
and beets.

Reader 3: Who cares what she was eating?

Reader 2: I care. If she's eating spinach and beets,
I'll be grossed out.

Reader 1: Can I just finish the rhyme?

Readers 2–5: Go ahead.

Little Miss Muffet

Reader's Theater *(cont.)*

Reader 1: Little Miss Muffet
Sat on a tuffet
Eating her curds and whey.
Along came a spider
And sat down beside her
And frightened Miss Muffet away.

Reader 2: The spider didn't scare her away.
It was the spinach and beets.

Reader 3: You don't know that it was
spinach and beets.

Reader 1: And you don't know that it
was milk and cookies. I'm glad
I'm finished with the rhyme.

Reader 5: Me, too.

Lock and Key

Standards

◎ Decode multisyllable words.

◎ Create engaging audio recordings of stories or poems that demonstrate fluid reading at an understandable pace.

◎ See Appendix C for additional standards.

Materials

◎ *Lock and Key* (page 64)

◎ *Lock and Key Word Ladder* (page 65)

◎ *Lock and Key Closed Word Sort* (page 66)

◎ *Lock and Key Rhyming Riddles* (page 67)

◎ *Lock and Key Reader's Theater* (pages 68–69)

Procedures

Introducing the Rhyme 🎤

1. Distribute the *Lock and Key* rhyme (page 64) to students.

2. Ask for two volunteers to read the rhyme orally, with each student reading every other line while the remainder of students follows along on their own scripts.

3. Divide the class into two groups. Read the rhyme chorally twice, allowing each group to take a turn at being the "don-key."

4. Allow students to illustrate the rhyme and add it to their individual poetry notebooks.

5. Have students add the title to their notebooks' tables of contents.

Word Ladder 🪜

1. Distribute *Lock and Key Word Ladder* (page 65) to students.

2. Tell them to follow your clues to make a word ladder from *lock* to *key*. Say the following:

   ◎ start at the bottom of the ladder—it keeps the door secure (*lock*)

   ◎ change the vowel—You are missing something. (*lack*)

   ◎ change the ending sound—a body of water (*lake*)

   ◎ change the beginning sound—when you create something (*make*)

   ◎ change one letter—a man or boy (*male*)

   ◎ change last two letters—another word for a lot (*many*)

   ◎ change the vowel and add a letter—you spend this (*money*)

   ◎ add one letter—a jungle animal (*monkey*)

   ◎ change one letter—a farm animal (*donkey*)

   ◎ remove three letters—It opens the lock. (*key*)

3. Help students make a meaningful connection between the poem and the first and last rungs of the ladder.

Lock and Key *(cont.)*

Closed Word Sort

1. Distribute sets of the *Lock and Key Closed Word Sort* cards (page 66) to individual students, pairs of students, or groups of students.

2. Have students sort the words according to the vowel sounds. Some words may belong in more than one group.

3. Follow the sorting with a discussion of word meanings and vowel rules.

4. Relate the words to the rhyme.

Rhyming Riddles

1. Have students think of as many words that rhyme with *lock* as they can. Have them tell their words to partners.

2. Distribute *Lock and Key Rhyming Riddles* (page 67) to students and make connections between the words students come up with in Step 1 with the words in the Word Bank.

3. Instruct students to use the words from the Word Bank to complete the riddles. Students can also create their own riddles for the words from the Word Bank or from the list of words they came up with in Step 1.

4. Have students illustrate one of the rhyming riddles on the backs of their papers.

Writing Connection

1. Have students brainstorm all the two-syllable words they can think of with *key* as the ending sound. The following words are provided as suggestions you can make if students get stuck, but students should be encouraged to come up with their own words.

> jockey (jock-key)
>
> icky (ick-key)
>
> ducky (duck-key)
>
> hockey (hock-key)
>
> wacky (wack-key)
>
> yucky (yuck-key)
>
> lucky (luck-key)
>
> tacky (tack-key)
>
> picky (pick-key)
>
> cookie (cook-key)
>
> stinky (stink-key)

2. Explain how to divide each word from the brainstormed list so that they can use the word *key* for each line. (See parentheses above.)

3. Have students write their own lock and key sequences, concluding with different humorous endings.

Reader's Theater

1. Distribute the *Lock and Key Reader's Theater* script (pages 68–69) to students.

2. Allow students to read the script independently.

3. Discuss the script.

4. Have students choose partners.

5. Allow several rehearsals to develop fluency.

6. Allow students to digitally record their script and take the recording home to share with family members.

Lock and Key

Traditional Rhyme

I am a gold lock.

I am a gold key.

I am a silver lock.

I am a silver key.

I am a brass lock.

I am a brass key.

I am a lead lock.

I am a lead key.

I am a don lock.

I am a don key!

Name: _____ Date: _____

Lock and Key

Word Ladder

· ·

Directions: Listen to the clues. Then, write the words on the rungs below as you climb the ladder.

10.

9.

8.

7.

6.

5.

4.

3.

2.

1.

Lock and Key

Closed Word Sort

Directions: Cut apart the cards. Then, sort them according to their vowel sounds.

lock	key	believe
ski	sleeve	prong
hog	hot	song
peace	tea	read
freeze	peacock	donkey
flock	dock	retrieve
stream	frost	belong
dog	steam	deep

Name: _____ Date: _____

Lock and Key

Rhyming Riddles

Directions: Use words from the Word Bank to complete the riddles below.
Note: You will not use all of the words.

Word Bank

flock	clock	shock
block	dock	sock
knocks	rock	mocks

1. a lock wearing a piece of clothing

   a lock in a _____

2. a lock looking for the time

   a lock checking the _____

3. a lock pounding on the door

   a lock that _____

4. a lock that is very surprised

   a lock in _____

5. a lock that makes fun of others

   a lock that _____

6. a lock ready for the beach

   a lock wearing sun_____

Lock and Key
Reader's Theater

All: Lock and Key

Reader 1: This looks like a really funny rhyme.

Reader 2: How so?

Reader 1: Well, I read one line that tells what kind of lock I am, and then you repeat the line except you say you're the key.

Reader 2: I'm not sure I understand.

Reader 1: Okay. Here's the first one. I say, "I am a gold lock." Then, you say, "I am a gold key." Every time I say what kind of lock I am, you say you're that same kind of key.

Reader 2: I think I know what you mean.

Reader 1: Okay. Here we go.
I am a gold lock.

Reader 2: I am a gold key.

Reader 1: I am a silver lock.

Reader 2: I am a silver key.

Reader 1: I am a brass lock.

Reader 2: I am a brass key.

Reader 1: I am a lead lock.

Reader 2: I am a lead key.

Reader 1: I am a don lock.

Reader 2: I am a don key.

Lock and Key
Reader's Theater (cont.)

Reader 1: Hah! That's really funny.

Reader 2: What's really funny?

Reader 1: You said you were a donkey.

Reader 2: I didn't think it was funny. Let me start one and you repeat after me.

Reader 1: Okay.

Reader 2: I am a tin lock.

Reader 1: I am a tin key.

Reader 2: I am a brass lock.

Reader 1: I am a brass key.

Reader 2: I am a round lock.

Reader 1: I am a round key.

Reader 2: I am a square lock.

Reader 1: I am a square key.

Reader 2: I am a mon lock.

Reader 1: I am a mon key.

Reader 2: Now, it's funny.

Little Bo Peep

Standards

- Decode multi-syllable words.
- Create engaging audio recordings of stories or poems that demonstrate fluid reading at an understandable pace.
- See Appendix C for additional standards.

Materials

- *Little Bo Peep* (page 72)
- *Little Bo Peep Word Ladder* (page 73)
- *Little Bo Peep Open Word Sort* (page 74)
- *Little Bo Peep Rhyming Riddles* (page 75)
- *Little Bo Peep Reader's Theater* (pages 76–78)

Procedures

Introducing the Rhyme

1. Distribute the *Little Bo Peep* rhyme (page 72) to students.

2. Use echo reading to develop fluency. Read the poem a line at a time. Have students repeat (echo read) after you. Encourage them to track print even if they can recite the poem from memory.

3. Allow students to illustrate the rhyme and add it to their individual poetry notebooks.

4. Have students add the title to their notebooks' tables of contents.

Word Ladder

1. Distribute *Little Bo Peep Word Ladder* (page 73) to students.

2. Tell them to follow your clues to make a word ladder from *sheep* to *lost*. Say the following:

   - start at the bottom of the ladder—what Little Bo Peep lost (*sheep*)
   - change the beginning sound—the sound a horn makes (*beep*)
   - change one letter—a dark red vegetable (*beet*)
   - change one letter—what you do to your opponent when you win a game (*beat*)
   - change one letter—a watercraft (*boat*)
   - change the beginning sound—what a boat does (*float*)
   - change the last two letters—You also do this when you brush your teeth. (*floss*)
   - take off one letter—opposite of a win is a _____ (*loss*)
   - change one letter—This describes Little Bo Peep's sheep. (*lost*)

3. Help students make a meaningful connection between the poem and the first and last rungs of the ladder.

Little Bo Peep *(cont.)*

Open Word Sort

1. Distribute sets of the *Little Bo Peep Open Word Sort* cards (page 74) to individual students, pairs of students, or groups of students.

2. Have students read the words and decide how they can be sorted. Encourage students to determine their own categories.

3. Follow the sorting with a discussion of word meanings and the different ways word groups were created.

4. Relate the words to the rhyme.

Rhyming Riddles

1. Have students think of as many words that rhyme with *sheep* as they can. Have them tell their words to partners.

2. Distribute *Little Bo Peep Rhyming Riddles* (page 75) to students and make connections between the words students come up with in Step 1 with the words in the Word Bank.

3. Instruct students to use the words from the Word Bank to complete the riddles. Students can also create their own riddles for the words from the Word Bank or from the list of words they came up with in Step 1.

4. Have students illustrate one of the rhyming riddles on the backs of their papers.

Writing Connection

1. Have students create "lost" posters advertising rewards for the return of Bo Peep's sheep. Tell students to make sure to include all relevant information: where the sheep were last seen, description of the sheep, and the amount of the reward.

2. Encourage students to connect ideas on the posters by using linking words (e.g., *also, another, and, more, but*).

Reader's Theater

1. Distribute the *Little Bo Peep Reader's Theater* script (pages 76–78) to students.

2. Allow students to read the script independently.

3. Discuss the script.

4. Assign parts for three readers.

5. Allow several rehearsals to develop fluency.

6. Digitally record the script and allow students to take the recording home to share with their family members.

Little Bo Peep

Traditional Rhyme

Little Bo Peep has lost her sheep

And doesn't know where to find them.

**Leave them alone and they'll
come home**

Wagging their tails behind them.

Name: _____ Date: _____

Little Bo Peep
Word Ladder

Directions: Listen to the clues. Then, write the words on the rungs below as you climb the ladder.

9.

8.

7.

6.

5.

4.

3.

2.

1.

Little Bo Peep

Open Word Sort

Directions: Cut apart the cards. Then, sort them into groups that you choose. Be ready to explain your groups.

sheep	shepherd	found
Bo Peep	pasture	sweaters
grass	wool	children
shear	wolf	lamb chops
meadow	Little Boy Blue	ram
Mary	fleece	tails
lamb	haystack	farm
school	asleep	flock
home	lost	ewe

Name: _____ Date: _____

Little Bo Peep

Rhyming Riddles

Directions: Use words from the Word Bank to complete the riddles below.
Note: You will not use all of the words.

Word Bank

peep	creep	jeep
beep	steep	deep
weep	sleep	keep

1. sheep riding in a 4-wheel drive vehicle

   sheep in a _____

2. sheep that are very tired

   sheep that _____

3. sheep with car horns

   sheep that _____

4. sheep who aren't in the shallow end

   sheep in the _____ end

5. sheep that are crying

   sheep that _____

6. sheep spying in the window

   sheep that _____

Little Bo Peep
Reader's Theater

All: Little Bo Peep

Reader 1: Little Bo Peep.

Reader 2: Who?

Reader 1: Little Bo Peep.

Reader 2: Who's that?
Does she go
to school here?

Reader 1: No, silly; she's the
character in
the rhyme.

Reader 3: Funny name.

Reader 1: Can I continue?

Reader 3: Sure. Go ahead.

Reader 1: Little Bo Peep has lost her sheep.

Reader 3: How does somebody lose sheep?

Reader 1: What?

Reader 3: People lose cats or lose dogs or even birds,
but I never heard of anyone losing sheep.
Aren't they kind of big to lose?

Reader 1: I don't know. It's a rhyme.
Can I please finish this?

Little Bo Peep

Reader's Theater (cont.)

Reader 3: Sure. Go ahead.

Reader 1: Little Bo Peep has lost her
sheep and doesn't know
where to find them.

Reader 2: What do you mean she doesn't know where to find them?
She must have some idea where they would be. I mean,
don't sheep eat grass? Wouldn't she look for them in a
place with lots and lots of grass?

Reader 1: I don't know. I don't even care. I just want to finish this
rhyme. Can I please finish the rhyme?

Reader 2: Sure. Go ahead.

Reader 1: Little Bo Peep has lost her sheep
And doesn't know where to find them.
Leave them alone and they'll come home.

Reader 3: Wait a minute. She's all worried about finding her sheep
and now we're all worried about finding her sheep, and
she's just going to give up and not search for them
anymore? That doesn't make any sense. I want her to
keep searching and searching until she finds them.
What if it gets dark and they run out in the road and get
hit by a car?

Little Bo Peep

Reader's Theater *(cont.)*

Reader 1: I don't care about the sheep anymore. I don't care if she ever finds them. All I want to do is finish this rhyme and be done with it. Will you please stop interrupting me and let me get finished with this?

Readers 2–3: Sure. Go ahead.

Reader 1: Little Bo Peep has lost her sheep
And doesn't know where to find them.
Leave them alone and they'll come home
Wagging their tails behind them.

Reader 2: Of course they'll be wagging their tails behind them.

Reader 3: They'll just be happy to be home, no thanks to her. What does she care? She's not lost. She's probably sitting at home watching television while the poor sheep are trying to find their way home. I'm leaving.

Reader 1: Where are you going?

Reader 3: I'm going to go out and find those lost sheep before they get hurt. And when I do find them, I'm going to take them home to that lazy Bo Peep and give her a piece of my mind.

Reader 1: I hate rhymes.

Me for Class President

Standards

◎ Refer to parts of stories, dramas, and poems when writing or speaking about a text, using terms such as chapter, scene, and stanza; describe how each successive part builds on earlier sections.

◎ Ask and answer questions to demonstrate understanding of a text, referring explicitly to the text as the basis for the answers.

◎ Create engaging audio recordings of stories or poems that demonstrate fluid reading at an understandable pace.

◎ See Appendix C for additional standards.

Materials

◎ *Me for Class President* (page 81)

◎ *Me for Class President Word Ladder* (page 82)

◎ *Me for Class President Open Word Sort* (page 83)

◎ *Me for Class President Rhyming Riddles* (page 84)

◎ *Me for Class President Reader's Theater* (page 85)

Procedures

Introducing the Rhyme 🎤

1. Distribute the *Me for Class President* rhyme (page 81) to students.

2. Discuss the term *stanza* with students. After listening to the rhyme, ask students to help detect the rhythm and rhyme that make up the stanzas.

3. Discuss the rhyme with students using the following questions:

    ◎ Who is speaking?

    ◎ What does the speaker want?

    ◎ What promises does the speaker make?

    ◎ Do you think she or he will keep those promises? Why or why not?

    ◎ Would you vote for this person? Why or why not?

4. Allow students to illustrate the rhyme and add it to their individual poetry notebooks.

5. Have students add the title to their notebooks' tables of contents.

Word Ladder 🪜

1. Distribute *Me for Class President Word Ladder* (page 82) to students.

2. Tell them to follow your clues to make a word ladder from *vote* to *me*. Say the following:

    ◎ start at the bottom of the ladder—what the speaker of the rhyme wants you to do (*vote*)

    ◎ change one letter—a brief letter (*note*)

    ◎ remove one letter—the second word in the contraction *don't* (*not*)

    ◎ change the beginning sound—something to cook in (*pot*)

    ◎ change the vowel—an animal that lives in your home (*pet*)

    ◎ change one consonant—a large aircraft (*jet*)

    ◎ change one letter—when you put something down (*set*)

    ◎ change one letter—what you do with your eyes (*see*)

    ◎ remove one letter and change one letter—a word for yourself (*me*)

3. Help students make a meaningful connection between the poem and the first and last rungs of the ladder.

Me for Class President *(cont.)*

Open Word Sort color size shape

1. Distribute sets of the *Me for Class President Open Word Sort* cards (page 83) to individual students, pairs of students, or groups of students.

2. Have students read the words and decide how they can be sorted. Encourage students to determine their own categories.

3. Follow the sorting with a discussion of word meanings and the different ways word groups were created.

4. Relate the words to the rhyme.

Rhyming Riddles ???

1. Have students think of as many words that rhyme with *vote* as they can. Have them tell their words to partners.

2. Distribute *Me for Class President Rhyming Riddles* (page 84) to students and make connections between the words students come up with in Step 1 and the words in the Word Bank.

3. Instruct students to use the words from the Word Bank to complete the riddles. Students can also create their own riddles for the words from the Word Bank or from the list of words they came up with in Step 1.

4. Have students illustrate one of the rhyming riddles on the backs of their papers.

Writing Connection

1. Have students create their own election posters telling why people should vote for them for class president.

2. Have students share their posters with the class.

Reader's Theater

1. Distribute the *Me for Class President Reader's Theater* script (page 85) to students.

2. Divide the class into three groups.

3. Assign each group a stanza of the poem.

4. Allow each group to rehearse its stanza several times to develop fluency.

5. Digitally record the final performance, and share the recording with another class.

Me for Class President

by Karen McGuigan Brothers

I'll give you the moon,

I'll give you the stars.

I'll fill up your desks

With sweet candy bars.

We'll start school at nine

And get out at noon,

No classes till March,

No more after June.

If you like my plan,

I know you can see

I'll give you good stuff

If you'll vote for me.

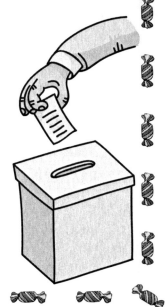

Name: _____ Date: _____

Me for Class President

Word Ladder

....

Directions: Listen to the clues. Then, write the words on the rungs below as you climb the ladder.

9. _____

8. _____

7. _____

6. _____

5. _____

4. _____

3. _____

2. _____

1. _____

#51339—Rhythm & Rhyme Literacy Time © *Shell Education*

Me for Class President

Open Word Sort

Directions: Cut apart the cards. Then, sort them into groups or categories that you choose. Be ready to explain your groups.

promise	vote
president	moon
stars	candy bars
candidate	school
March	June
November	noon
election	speech
class	campaign

Name: _____ Date: _____

Me for Class President

Rhyming Riddles

Directions: Use words from the Word Bank to complete the riddles below.
Note: You will not use all of the words.

Word Bank

float	boat	gloat
throat	goat	moat
quote	note	coat

1. You vote when it is cold.

   vote wearing a _____

2. You vote when you are sick.

   vote with a sore _____

3. You vote on a watercraft.

   vote on a _____

4. You vote with a farm animal.

   vote with a _____

5. You vote and repeat something someone said.

   vote and say a _____

6. You write your vote on a small piece of paper.

   vote with a _____

Me for Class President

Reader's Theater

All: Me for Class President

Group 1: I'll give you the moon,

I'll give you the stars.

I'll fill up your desks

With sweet candy bars.

Group 2: We'll start school at nine

And get out at noon,

No classes till March,

No more after June.

Group 3: If you like my plan,

I know you can see

I'll give you good stuff

If you'll vote for me.

Old Mother Hubbard

Standards

- Refer to parts of stories, dramas, and poems when writing or speaking about a text, using terms such as chapter, scene, and stanza; describe how each successive part builds on earlier sections.

- Determine the meaning of words and phrases as they are used in a text, distinguishing literal from non-literal language.

- Use glossaries and beginning dictionaries, both print and digital, to determine or clarify the precise meaning of key words and phrases.

- See Appendix C for additional standards.

Materials

- *Old Mother Hubbard* (page 88)

- *Old Mother Hubbard Word Ladder* (page 89)

- *Old Mother Hubbard Closed Word Sort* (page 90)

- *Old Mother Hubbard Rhyming Riddles* (page 91)

- *Old Mother Hubbard Reader's Theater* (pages 92–94)

Procedures

Introducing the Rhyme

1. Distribute the *Old Mother Hubbard* rhyme (page 88) to students.

2. Ask students to follow along as you read the rhyme aloud.

3. Divide the class into four groups, and assign each group a stanza to read. Groups can be created by birth dates (January through March, April through June, etc.), clothing colors, hair colors, and so on. Students will enjoy suggesting how groups can be formed.

4. Read the rhyme several times for fluency, changing the groupings so that students get practice with different stanzas.

5. Guide students in using context clues to determine the meaning of the following words: *curtsy, hatter, tailor, jig,* and *dame.* Ask for volunteers to verify the meanings with the use of a dictionary or online resource.

6. Allow students to illustrate the rhyme and add it to their individual poetry notebooks.

7. Have students add the title to their notebooks' tables of contents.

Word Ladder

1. Distribute *Old Mother Hubbard Word Ladder* (page 89) to students.

2. Tell them to follow your clues to make a word ladder from *dog* to *bone.* Say the following:

   - start at the bottom of the ladder—Mother Hubbard's pet (*dog*)

   - change one letter—a small mark made by your pencil (*dot*)

   - change one letter—something you can sleep on (*cot*)

   - change one letter—something you cook in (*pot*)

   - change one letter—you won't do something; I will _____. (*not*)

   - rearrange the letters—2,000 pounds (*ton*)

   - add one letter—a sound in music (*tone*)

   - change the beginning sound—you can call your friends with this (*phone*)

   - change the beginning sound—what Mother Hubbard went to get (*bone*)

3. Help students make a meaningful connection between the poem and the first and last rungs of the ladder.

Old Mother Hubbard *(cont.)*

Closed Word Sort

1. Distribute sets of the *Old Mother Hubbard Closed Word Sort* cards (page 90) to individual students, pairs of students, or groups of students.

2. Have students sort their words according to short and long vowels. After the initial sort, have them further sort them according to vowel rules (e.g., CVC, CVVC, CVCe).

3. Follow the sorting with a discussion of word meanings and vowel rules.

4. Relate the words to the rhyme.

Rhyming Riddles

1. Have students think of as many words that rhyme with *dog* as they can. Have them tell their words to partners.

2. Distribute *Old Mother Hubbard Rhyming Riddles* (page 91) to students and make connections between the words students come up with in Step 1 with the words in the Word Bank.

3. Instruct students to use the words from the Word Bank to complete the riddles. Students can also create their own riddles for the words from the Word Bank or from the list of words they came up with in Step 1.

4. Have students illustrate one of the rhyming riddles on the backs of their papers.

Writing Connection

1. Divide students into pairs.

2. Have students work with partners to write a dialogue between Mother Hubbard and the dog.

3. Allow time to rehearse, and then have pairs perform their scripts for the class.

Reader's Theater

1. Distribute the *Old Mother Hubbard Reader's Theater* script (pages 92–94) to students.

2. Allow students to read the script independently.

3. Discuss the script.

4. Assign parts for five readers.

5. Allow each group to rehearse its stanza several times to develop fluency.

6. Perform the reader's theater for the class, another class, or for a special school event.

Old Mother Hubbard

Traditional Rhyme

Old Mother Hubbard
Went to the cupboard
To get her poor dog
   a bone.
But when she
   got there,
The cupboard
   was bare
And so the poor dog
   had none.

She went to
   the hatter's
To buy him a hat;
When she came back,
He was feeding the cat.

She went to
   the barber's
To buy him a wig,
And when she got back
He was dancing a jig.

She went to the tailor's
To buy him a coat,
And when she got back
He was riding a goat.

The dame made
   a curtsy,
The dog made a bow;
The dame said,
   "Your servant."
The dog said
   "Bow-wow."

Name: _____ Date: _____

Old Mother Hubbard

Word Ladder

· ·

Directions: Listen to the clues. Then, write the words on the rungs below as you climb the ladder.

9.

8.

7.

6.

5.

4.

3.

2.

1.

Old Mother Hubbard

Closed Word Sort

Directions: Cut apart the cards. Then, sort them into groups according to short and long vowels.

goat	**old**	**jig**
coat	**bare**	**dog**
bone	**dame**	**say**
phone	**nice**	**rhyme**
lady	**wait**	**wig**
list	**yes**	**get**
back	**cat**	**bone**

Name: _____ Date: _____

Old Mother Hubbard

Rhyming Riddles

∙ ∙

Directions: Use words from the Word Bank to complete the riddles below.
Note: You will not use all of the words.

Word Bank

fog	blog	frogs
togs	logs	clog
bogs	jog	hogs

1. dogs that run around the track

   dogs that _____

2. dogs in misty weather

   dogs in _____

3. dogs playing with amphibians

   dogs playing with _____

4. dogs sitting on tree branches

   dogs on _____

5. dogs on the Internet

   dogs that _____

6. dogs kissing pigs

   dogs kissing _____

Old Mother Hubbard

Reader's Theater

All: Old Mother Hubbard

Reader 1: Old Mother Hubbard
Went to the cupboard
To get her poor dog a bone.

Reader 2: That's nice.

Reader 1: What did you say?

Reader 2: That's nice.

Reader 1: What's nice?

Reader 2: It's nice that the little
old lady went to the
cupboard to get her dog
a bone.

Reader 1: Wait. I'm not done.

Old Mother Hubbard
Went to the cupboard
To get her poor dog a bone.
But when she got there,
The cupboard was bare
And so the poor dog had none.

Reader 3: What?! She forgot to get her dog some bones?! What's the
matter with her, anyway? Did she forget to put them on her
grocery list?

Reader 1: Let me finish the rhyme.

Old Mother Hubbard

Reader's Theater *(cont.)*

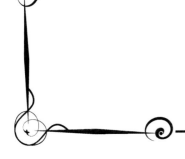

Reader 3: There's more?

Reader 1: Yes.

She went to the hatter's to buy him a hat;
When she came back, he was feeding the cat.

Reader 3: Oh, I see. So she remembered to buy the cat some food, but not some bones for the dog. And why was she out buying him a hat? All he wants is a bone.

Reader 1: Let's finish this.

She went to the barber's
To buy him a wig,
And when she got back
He was dancing a jig.

Reader 4: He wasn't dancing! He was jumping around to get her to understand that he doesn't want a stupid hat or a stupid wig; all he wants is a bone. Why is she buying all this other stuff?

Reader 1: Here's some more:

She went to the tailor's
To buy him a coat,
And when she got back
He was riding a goat.

Reader 4: For crying out loud! He was probably trying to ride the goat to town to get his own bone. He needs to reject the coat. Maybe if he puts it on the goat, the woman will understand that he just wants a bone. No coat. . . just a bone.

Old Mother Hubbard

Reader's Theater (cont.)

Reader 1: Here's the end:

The dame made a curtsy,
The dog made a bow;
The dame said, "Your servant."
The dog said "Bow-wow."

Reader 5: The dog wasn't bowing. He was putting his head down out of sheer frustration because he couldn't make her understand that all he wanted was a bone.

Reader 2: How would you have ended the rhyme?

Reader 5: Like this:

The dame made a curtsy,
Then picked up the phone
And ordered the dog
A big juicy bone.

Reader 3: I like it.

Reader 5: Thanks.

For Want of a Nail

Standards

- Determine the main ideas and supporting details of a text read aloud or information presented in diverse media and formats, including visually, quantitatively, and orally.

- Write narratives to develop real or imagined experiences or events using effective technique, descriptive details, and clear event sequences.

- See Appendix C for additional standards.

Materials

- *For Want of a Nail* (page 97)
- *For Want of a Nail Word Ladder* (page 98)
- *For Want of a Nail Closed Word Sort* (page 99)
- *For Want of a Nail Rhyming Riddles* (page 100)
- *For Want of a Nail Reader's Theater* (pages 101–102)

Procedures

Introducing the Rhyme

1. Distribute the *For Want of a Nail* rhyme (page 97) to students.

2. Read the rhyme chorally several times to develop fluency.

3. Discuss the setting of the rhyme.

4. Discuss the sequence of cause and effect events that lead to the main idea.

5. Allow students to illustrate the rhyme and add it to their individual poetry notebooks.

6. Have students add the title to their notebooks' tables of contents.

Word Ladder

1. Distribute *For Want of a Nail Word Ladder* (page 98) to students.

2. Tell them to follow your clues to make a word ladder from *want* to *nail*. Say the following:

   - start at the bottom of the ladder—*For _____ of a nail* (*want*)
   - change one letter—Magicians use this for making magic. (*wand*)
   - remove one letter—This word means *also*. (*and*)
   - change one letter—This insect can spoil your picnic. (*ant*)
   - rearrange the letters—what you get when you sit in the sun (*tan*)
   - change one letter—You moved fast with your legs. (*ran*)
   - add one letter—another word for *precipitation* (*rain*)
   - add one letter—a type of transportation (*train*)
   - change one letter—a place to hike (*trail*)
   - change the beginning sound—The kingdom was lost because this was missing. (*nail*)

3. Help students make a meaningful connection between the poem and the first and last rungs of the ladder.

For Want of a Nail *(cont.)*

Closed Word Sort

1. Divide students into small groups.

2. Distribute sets of the *For Want of a Nail Closed Word Sort* cards (page 99) to each group of students.

3. Explain to students that they will create their own word sort this time. They will need to fill in their blank cards to create a word sort for other groups. As a class, brainstorm categories of ideas they can create (e.g., parts of speech, numbers of syllables, phonics rules).

4. Have teams exchange their cards and sort them.

5. Follow the sorting with a discussion of word meanings and different ways groups were created.

Rhyming Riddles

1. Have students think of as many words that rhyme with *shoe* as they can. Have them tell their words to partners.

2. Distribute *For Want of a Nail Rhyming Riddles* (page 100) to students and make connections between the words students come up with in Step 1 with the words in the Word Bank.

3. Instruct students to use the words from the Word Bank to complete the riddles. Students can also create their own riddles for the words from the Word Bank or from the list of words they came up with in Step 1.

4. Have students illustrate one of the rhyming riddles on the backs of their papers.

Writing Connection

1. There are many children's books that demonstrate cause and effect through a chain of events (e.g., *If You Give a Mouse a Cookie, The House that Jack Built*). Ask your school librarian to join the class in searching for such books.

2. Write a class story that follows the cause/effect pattern. Let students illustrate each page.

3. Have teams of students practice reading the book aloud. Send the teams to other classes to share.

Reader's Theater

1. Distribute the *For Want of a Nail Reader's Theater* script (pages 101–102) to students.

2. Allow students to read the script independently.

3. Discuss the script.

4. Assign parts for five readers.

5. Allow each group to rehearse its stanza several times to develop fluency.

6. Perform the reader's theater for the class, another class, or for a special school event.

For Want of a Nail

Traditional Rhyme

For want of a nail,
the shoe was lost;

For want of the shoe,
the horse was lost;

For want of the horse,
the rider was lost;

For want of the rider,
the battle was lost;

For want of the battle,
the kingdom was lost;

And all for the want of a
horseshoe nail.

Name: _____ Date: _____

For Want of a Nail

Word Ladder

....

Directions: Listen to the clues. Then, write the words on the rungs below as you climb the ladder.

10.

9.

8.

7.

6.

5.

4.

3.

2.

1.

For Want of a Nail

Closed Word Sort

Directions: Cut apart the cards. For this activity, you will work in a team to create a word sort for another team. You have been provided several word cards to include in your word sort. Fill in the blank word cards and identify the category for your classmates.

nail	**shoe**
horse	**rider**
battle	**kingdom**
lost	

Name: _____ Date: _____

For Want of a Nail

Rhyming Riddles

Directions: Use words from the Word Bank to complete the riddles below.
Note: You will not use all of the words.

Word Bank

few	zoo	new
chew	dew	glue
stew	blue	grew

1. a horseshoe that got bigger

   a horseshoe that _____

2. a horseshoe that was just purchased

   a horseshoe that is _____

3. a horseshoe that needs to be repaired

   a horseshoe that needs some _____

4. a horseshoe in a place where there are caged animals

   a horseshoe at the _____

5. a horseshoe that is the color of the sky

   a horseshoe that is _____

6. a horseshoe that stepped in the wet grass

   a horseshoe in the _____

For Want of a Nail

Reader's Theater

All: For Want of a Nail

Reader 1:   This is a rhyme about how one little thing can affect bigger things.

Reader 2:   What one little thing?

Reader 1:   Let me read it.

For want of a nail, the shoe was lost.

Reader 3:   My mom had fake nails put on once, and she lost a nail and it affected something bigger.

Reader 4:   What did it affect?

Reader 3:   Her whole hand. It looked really strange with four long nails and one short nail.

Reader 1:   Yes, but the nail that was lost in the rhyme made somebody lose a shoe.

Reader 5:   Must have been a toenail. Yuck! I never heard of fake toenails.

Reader 1:   The nail in the rhyme wasn't that kind of a nail.

Reader 5:   What kind was it?

Reader 1:   It was a horseshoe nail that was on a horse.

Reader 5:   Do they put horseshoes on a horse with nails?

Reader 1:   Yes.

Reader 4:   Doesn't that hurt?

For Want of a Nail

Reader's Theater (cont.)

Reader 1: No. A horse's hooves are very hard and the horseshoes actually protect them from wearing down and making the horse lame.

Reader 2: Tell us more about the horseshoe in the rhyme.

Reader 1: Okay.

For want of a nail, the shoe was lost;
For want of the shoe, the horse was lost;

Reader 3: Why did the lost shoe make the horse lost?

Reader 1: Probably because the horseshoe came off and the horse could no longer be ridden.

Reader 3: That makes sense. Read the whole rhyme.

Reader 1: For want of a nail, the shoe was lost;
For want of the shoe, the horse was lost;
For want of the horse, the rider was lost;
For want of the rider, the battle was lost;
For want of the battle, the kingdom was lost;
And all for the want of a horseshoe nail.

Reader 2: Wow! You would think that if a horseshoe was that important, the rider would carry a hammer and some nails.

Reader 3: It would have been a lot cheaper than losing a whole kingdom.

Anna Maria

Standards

- Determine the main ideas and supporting details of a text read aloud or information presented in diverse media and formats, including visually, quantitatively, and orally.
- Know and apply grade-level phonics and word analysis skills in decoding words.
- See Appendix C for additional standards.

Materials

- *Anna Maria* (page 105)
- *Anna Maria Word Ladder* (page 106)
- *Anna Maria Open Word Sort* (page 107)
- *Anna Maria Rhyming Riddles* (page 108)
- *Anna Maria Reader's Theater* (page 109)

Procedures

Introducing the Rhyme

1. Distribute the *Anna Maria* rhyme (page 105) to students.
2. Ask students to read the rhyme silently.
3. Discuss the sequence of cause and effect events that lead to the main idea.
4. Discuss how the rhyme's sequence compares to that of *For Want of a Nail* in Lesson 11.
5. Allow students to illustrate the rhyme and add it to their individual poetry notebooks.
6. Have students add the title to their notebooks' tables of contents.

Word Ladder

1. Distribute *Anna Maria Word Ladder* (page 106) to students.
2. Tell them to follow your clues to make a word ladder from *fire* to *pot*. Say the following:
   - start at the bottom of the ladder—the first thing Anna Maria sat on (*fire*)
   - change one consonant—This is how Anna Maria felt before she sat on the fire. (*fine*)
   - remove one letter—This is on a fish. (*fin*)
   - change one letter—a small, sharp object (*pin*)
   - add one letter—a type of tree (*pine*)
   - change one vowel—the glass in a window (*pane*)
   - remove one letter—used for cooking (*pan*)
   - change one consonant—to touch lightly on the head (*pat*)
   - change one letter—something you use to boil water (*pot*)
3. Help students make a meaningful connection between the poem and the first and last rungs of the ladder.

Anna Maria *(cont.)*

Open Word Sort

1. Distribute sets of the *Anna Maria Open Word Sort* cards (page 107) to individual students, pairs of students, or groups of students.

2. Have students read the words and decide how they can be sorted. Have students add at least three words of their own that will fit into the categories.

3. Follow the sorting with a discussion of word meanings and the different ways word groups were created.

4. Relate the words to the rhyme.

Rhyming Riddles

1. Have students think of as many words that rhyme with *fire* as they can. Have them tell their words to partners.

2. Distribute *Anna Maria Rhyming Riddles* (page 108) to students and make connections between the words students come up with in Step 1 with the words in the Word Bank.

3. Instruct students to use the words from the Word Bank to complete the riddles. Students can also create their own riddles for the words from the Word Bank or from the list of words they came up with in Step 1.

4. Have students illustrate one of the rhyming riddles on the backs of their papers.

Writing Connection

1. As a class, generate a list of all the things Anna Maria could sit on. Have students create new rhymes based on the following format:

   Anna Maria she sat on a ____A____.

   The ____A____ was too ____B____, she sat on a ____C____.

   Words in spaces *B* and *C* should rhyme.

Example
Anna Maria she sat on a boy;
The boy was too coy, she sat on a toy;
The toy was too hard, she sat in the lard;
The lard was too slick, she sat on a stick.

2. Have students share their new rhymes with the class.

Reader's Theater

1. Distribute the *Anna Maria Reader's Theater* script (page 109) to students.

2. Allow students to read the script independently.

3. Discuss the script.

4. Assign parts for five readers.

5. Allow several rehearsals to develop fluency.

6. Perform the reader's theater for the class, another class, or for a special school event.

Anna Maria

Traditional Rhyme

Anna Maria
    she sat on the fire;

The fire was too hot,
    she sat on the pot;

The pot was too round,
    she sat on the ground;

The ground was too flat,
    she sat on the cat;

The cat ran away with Maria on her back.

Name: _____ Date: _____

Anna Maria

Word Ladder

. . . .

Directions: Listen to the clues. Then, write the words on the rungs below as you climb the ladder.

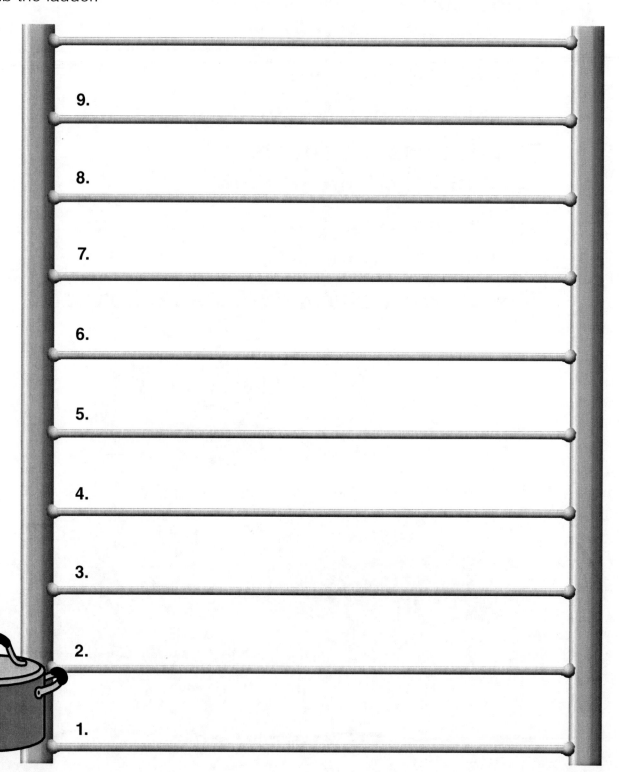

Anna Maria

Open Word Sort

Directions: Cut apart the cards. Then, sort them into groups or categories that you choose. Add at least three words that you choose. Be ready to explain your groups.

Anna	**cat**
Maria	**ground**
pot	**hot**
sat	**round**
flat	**ran**
back	**fire**

Name: _____ Date: _____

Anna Maria

Rhyming Riddles

· ·

Directions: Use words from the Word Bank to complete the riddles below.
Note: You will not use all of the words.

Word Bank

wire	fire	liar
hire	retire	tire
sapphire	umpire	higher

1. Anna Maria sat where it was hot.

   Anna Maria sat on the _____.

2. Anna Maria will call strikes at a baseball game.

   Anna Maria is an _____.

3. Anna Maria will quit working when she gets old.

   Anna Maria will _____.

4. Anna Maria always tells the truth.

   Anna Maria is not a _____.

5. Anna Maria wants to climb to the top.

   Anna Maria wants to go _____.

6. Anna Maria wants a blue gemstone.

   Anna Maria wants a _____.

Anna Maria

Reader's Theater

All: Here is a rhyme called *Anna Maria.*

Reader 1:   Anna Maria

All: she sat on the fire;

Reader 2:   The fire was too hot,

All: she sat on the pot;

Reader 3:   The pot was too round,

All: she sat on the ground;

Reader 4:   The ground was too flat,

All: she sat on the cat;

Reader 5:   The cat ran away

All: with Maria on her back.

Miss Mary Mack

Standards

◎ Ask and answer questions to demonstrate understanding of a text, referring explicitly to the text as the basis for the answers.

◎ Read with sufficient accuracy and fluency to support comprehension.

◎ Use glossaries or beginning dictionaries, both print and digital, to determine or clarify the precise meaning of key words and phrases.

◎ See Appendix C for additional standards.

Materials

◎ *Miss Mary Mack* (page 112)

◎ *Miss Mary Mack Word Ladder* (page 113)

◎ *Miss Mary Mack Open Word Sort* (page 114)

◎ *Miss Mary Mack Rhyming Riddles* (page 115)

◎ *Miss Mary Mack Reader's Theater* (page 116)

Procedures

Introducing the Rhyme

1. Distribute the *Miss Mary Mack* rhyme (page 112) to students.

2. Ask students to read the rhyme silently.

3. Discuss the cause and effect events in the rhyme.

4. Ask for volunteers to read the rhyme.

5. Read the rhyme chorally.

6. Allow students to illustrate the rhyme and add it to their individual poetry notebooks.

7. Have students add the title to their notebooks' tables of contents.

Word Ladder

1. Distribute *Miss Mary Mack Word Ladder* (page 113) to students.

2. Tell them to follow your clues to make a word ladder from *Mary* to *Mack*. Say the following:

   ◎ start at the bottom of the ladder—the first name of the girl in the rhyme (*Mary*)

   ◎ change one letter—a female horse (*mare*)

   ◎ remove one letter—to damage something (*mar*)

   ◎ change one letter—a sticky black substance (*tar*)

   ◎ change one letter—a container for food (*jar*)

   ◎ change one letter—fruit to spread on bread (*jam*)

   ◎ change the ending sound—_____and Jill (*Jack*)

   ◎ change one consonant—to be missing something (*lack*)

   ◎ change one letter—a small, sharp object (*tack*)

   ◎ change the first letter—last name of the girl in the rhyme (*Mack*)

3. Help students make a meaningful connection between the poem and the first and last rungs of the ladder.

Miss Mary Mack *(cont.)*

Open Word Sort

1. Distribute sets of the *Miss Mary Mack Open Word Sort* cards (page 114) to individual students, pairs of students, or groups of students.

2. Have students read the words and decide how they can be sorted.

3. Follow the sorting with a discussion of word meanings and the different ways word groups were created.

4. Relate the words to the rhyme.

Rhyming Riddles

1. Ask students to think of compound words that end in *ack*. In order to answer the riddles, students will need to define some of the words they locate. Allow students to use technology to define the words.

2. Distribute *Miss Mary Mack Rhyming Riddles* (page 115) to students and make meaningful connections between the words students come up with in Step 1 with the words in the Word Bank.

3. Instruct students to use the words from the Word Bank to complete the riddles. Students can also create their own riddles for the words from the Word Bank or from the list of words they came up with in Step 1.

4. Have students illustrate one of the rhyming riddles on the backs of their papers.

Writing Connection

1. Have students create copy changes for the poem. Copy change is a writing activity where the writer borrows the structure of another text and uses it as a skeleton for his or her own piece. Poetry or stories written in verse are frequently used as copy change texts. Because key words are changed, the new piece takes on its own identity, which is different from the original.

2. Instruct students to use the following format as they create their copy changes:

   She went _____ to _____,

   She made a mistake and _____.

Example
She went to town to buy a gown,
She made a mistake and got a clown.

3. Have students share their new rhymes with the class.

Reader's Theater

1. Distribute the *Miss Mary Mack Reader's Theater* script (page 116) to students.

2. Allow students to read the script independently.

3. Discuss the script.

4. Assign parts for eight readers.

5. Allow several rehearsals to develop fluency.

6. Perform the reader's theater for the class, another class, or for a special school event.

Miss Mary Mack

Traditional Rhyme

Miss Mary Mack, Mack, Mack,

All dressed in black, black, black,

With silver buttons, buttons, buttons,

All down her back, back, back.

She went upstairs to make her bed,

She made a mistake and
    bumped her head;

She went downstairs
    to wash the dishes,

She made a mistake
    and washed her
    wishes;

She went outside to
    hang her clothes,

She made a mistake and
    hung her nose.

Name: _____ Date: _____

Miss Mary Mack

Word Ladder

· ·

Directions: Listen to the clues. Then, write the words on the rungs below as you climb the ladder.

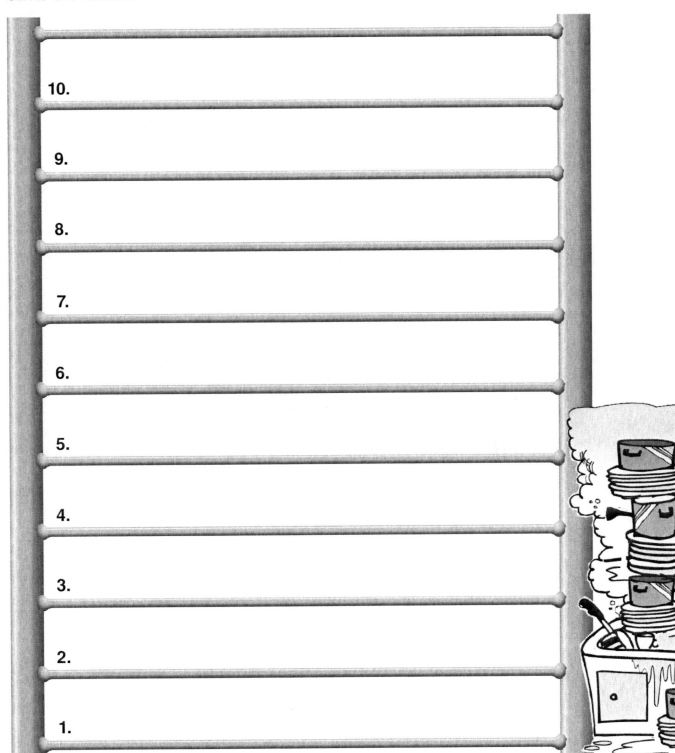

10.

9.

8.

7.

6.

5.

4.

3.

2.

1.

Miss Mary Mack

Open Word Sort

Directions: Cut apart the cards. Then, sort them into groups or categories that you choose. Be ready to explain your groups.

Mary	**Mack**
black	**buttons**
silver	**back**
upstairs	**bed**
head	**mistakes**
wishes	**dishes**
clothes	**outside**
nose	**downstairs**

Name: _____ Date: _____

Miss Mary Mack

Rhyming Riddles

Directions: Use words from the Word Bank to complete the riddles below.
Note: You will not use all of the words.

Word Bank

quarterback	pullback	wisecrack
backpack	unpack	flashback
backtrack	piggyback	retrack

1. Miss Mary Mack carries books on her back.

   Miss Mary Mack has a _____ .

2. Miss Mary Mack has to retrace her steps.

   Miss Mary Mack has to _____ .

3. Miss Mary Mack is carried upon her dad's back.

   Miss Mary Mack gets a _____ ride.

4. Miss Mary Mack plays football.

   Miss Mary Mack is a _____ .

5. Miss Mary Mack made a sassy remark.

   Miss Mary Mack made a _____ .

6. Miss Mary Mack remembers an old memory.

   Miss Mary Mack has a _____ moment.

Miss Mary Mack

Reader's Theater

All: Miss Mary Mack

Reader 1:   Miss Mary Mack, Mack, Mack,

Readers 1–2:   All dressed in black, black, black,

Readers 1–3:   With silver buttons, buttons, buttons,

All: All down her back, back, back.

Reader 4:   She went upstairs to make her bed,

Reader 5:   She made a mistake and bumped her head;

Reader 6:   She went downstairs to wash the dishes,

Reader 7:   She made a mistake and washed her wishes;

Reader 8:   She went outside to hang her clothes,

All: She made a mistake and hung her nose.

Peter Piper

Standards

- Use glossaries or beginning dictionaries, both print and digital, to determine or clarify the precise meaning of key words and phrases.
- Explain the function of nouns, pronouns, verbs, adjectives, and adverbs in general and their functions in particular sentences.
- Create engaging audio recordings of stories or poems that demonstrate fluid reading at an understandable pace.
- See Appendix C for additional standards.

Materials

- *Peter Piper* (page 119)
- *Peter Piper Word Ladder* (page 120)
- *Peter Piper Closed Word Sort* (page 121)
- *Peter Piper Rhyming Riddles* (page 122)
- *Peter Piper Reader's Theater* (page 123)

Procedures

Introducing the Rhyme

1. Distribute the *Peter Piper* rhyme (page 119) to students.
2. Ask students to read the rhyme silently.
3. Show students online videos of people and other characters reciting the rhyme.
4. Have students use dictionaries or online resources to define the following words: *peck*, *pickled*, and *peppers*.
5. Model the rhyme and read aloud as fluently as possible.
6. Allow students to practice the rhyme with partners.
7. Allow students to illustrate the rhyme and add it to their individual poetry notebooks.
8. Have students add the title to their notebooks' tables of contents.

Word Ladder

1. Distribute *Peter Piper Word Ladder* (page 120) to students.
2. Tell them to follow your clues to make a word ladder from *Peter* to *pickled*. Say the following:
   - start at the bottom of the ladder—the first name of the boy in the rhyme (*Peter*)
   - remove one consonant—a nickname for the boy (*Pete*)
   - remove one vowel—an animal that lives in your home (*pet*)
   - change one letter—another word for a peach seed (*pit*)
   - change one consonant—a small, sharp object (*pin*)
   - change the ending sound—what Peter will do with the peppers (*pick*)
   - add an ending—past tense of the verb in Number 6 (*picked*)
   - add one consonant—the kind of peppers Peter picked (*pickled*)
3. Help students make a meaningful connection between the poem and the first and last rungs of the ladder.

Peter Piper *(cont.)*

Closed Word Sort

1. Divide students into small groups.

2. Distribute sets of the *Peter Piper Closed Word Sort* cards (page 121) to each group of students.

3. Explain to students that they will need to fill in their blank cards to create a word sort for other groups. As a class, brainstorm categories of ideas they can create (e.g., parts of speech, number of syllables, phonics rules).

4. Have teams exchange their cards and sort them.

5. Follow the sorting with a discussion of word meanings and different ways groups were created.

Rhyming Riddles

1. Have students think of as many words that rhyme with *pick* as they can. Have them tell their words to partners.

2. Distribute *Peter Piper Rhyming Riddles* (page 122) to students and make connections between the words students come up with in Step 1 with the words in the Word Bank.

3. Instruct students to use the words from the Word Bank to complete the riddles. Students can also create their own riddles for the words from the Word Bank or from the list of words they came up with in Step 1.

4. Have students illustrate one of the rhyming riddles on the backs of their papers.

Writing Connection

1. Have each student choose five consonants.

2. Brainstorm lists of nouns, verbs, adjectives, and adverbs for each consonant.

3. Choose words from each list to make tongue-twister sentences.

4. Share with the class.

5. Challenge one another to a tongue-twister contest.

Reader's Theater

1. Distribute the *Peter Piper Reader's Theater* script (page 123) to students.

2. Allow students to read the script independently.

3. Have students indicate the assigned parts on their scripts.

4. Allow several rehearsals to develop fluency.

5. Allow students to digitally record their script and take the recording home to share with family members.

Peter Piper

Traditional Rhyme

Peter Piper picked a peck
  of pickled peppers;

A peck of pickled peppers
  Peter Piper picked;

If Peter Piper picked a
  peck of pickled peppers,

Where's the peck of pickled
  peppers Peter Piper picked?

If Peter Piper picked a peck
  of pickled peppers

Were they pickled when he
  picked them off the vine?

Or was Peter Piper
  peppered as he picked
  the pickled peppers,

Picked the peppers from
  the pickled pepper vine?

Name: _____ Date: _____

Peter Piper

Word Ladder

. . . .

Directions: Listen to the clues. Then, write the words on the rungs below as you climb the ladder.

8.

7.

6.

5.

4.

3.

2.

1.

Peter Piper

Closed Word Sort

Directions: Cut apart the cards. Then, fill in the blank word cards with more words that you choose to create a closed word sort for another group of students. Identify the category for your classmates.

peck	peppers
Peter	picked

Name: _____ Date: _____

Peter Piper

Rhyming Riddles

Directions: Use words from the Word Bank to complete the riddles below.
Note: You will not use all of the words.

Word Bank

tricks	slick	sick
thick	lick	stick
quick	wick	chick

1. a pickle-flavored ice cream cone

a pickle you _____

2. a pickle dancing with a baby chicken

a pickle dancing with a _____

3. a pickle that needs a doctor

a pickle that is _____

4. a fast pickle

a pickle that is _____

5. a pickle doing a magic show

a pickle doing _____

6. a pickle on a small tree branch

a pickle on a _____

Peter Piper

Reader's Theater

_____ : Peter Piper

_____ : Peter Piper picked a peck of pickled peppers;

_____ : A peck of pickled peppers Peter Piper picked;

_____ : If Peter Piper picked a peck of pickled peppers,

_____ : Where's the peck of pickled peppers Peter Piper picked?

_____ : If Peter Piper picked a peck of pickled peppers

_____ : Were they pickled when he picked them off the vine?

_____ : Or was Peter Piper peppered as he picked the pickled peppers,

_____ : Picked the peppers from the pickled pepper vine?

The Monster Under My Bed

Standards

- Read grade-level appropriate irregularly spelled words.
- Write narratives to develop real or imagined experiences or events using effective technique, descriptive details, and clear event sequences.
- Explain the function of nouns, pronouns, verbs, adjectives, and adverbs in general and their function in particular sentences.
- See Appendix C for additional standards.

Materials

- *The Monster Under My Bed* (page 126)
- *The Monster Under My Bed Word Ladder* (page 127)
- *The Monster Under My Bed Closed Word Sort* (page 128)
- *The Monster Under My Bed Rhyming Riddles* (page 129)
- *The Monster Under My Bed Reader's Theater* (pages 130–133)

Procedures

Introducing the Rhyme

1. Distribute *The Monster Under My Bed* rhyme (page 126) to students.

2. Ask students to read the rhyme silently.

3. Discuss the poem with students.

4. Allow students to illustrate the rhyme and add it to their individual poetry notebooks.

5. Have students add the title to their notebooks' tables of contents.

Word Ladder

1. Distribute *The Monster Under My Bed Word Ladder* (page 127) to students.

2. Tell them to follow your clues to make a word ladder from *Fred* to *bed*. Say the following:

   - start at the bottom of the ladder—the monster's name (*Fred*)
   - change the beginning sound—to get married (*wed*)
   - add one vowel—a plant that doesn't belong in the garden (*weed*)
   - change one consonant—how a plant begins (*seed*)
   - change one consonant—to give your pet his food (*feed*)
   - change one consonant—where you put your shoes (*feet*)
   - change one consonant—a dark red vegetable (*beet*)
   - remove one letter—you are sure you can win (*bet*)
   - change one letter—what the monster lived under (*bed*)

3. Help students make a meaningful connection between the poem and the first and last rungs of the ladder.

The Monster Under My Bed (cont.)

Closed Word Sort

1. Distribute sets of *The Monster Under My Bed Closed Word Sort* cards (page 128) to each group of students.

2. Review the following terms with students: *noun*, *verb*, *adjective*, *pronoun*, and *adverb*.

3. Have students sort their words according to the part of speech each word represents. Explain to students that some words could be placed in more than one group. Have them refer to the poem as they sort to verify how the word is used.

4. Follow the sorting with a discussion of words and their functions in the poem.

Rhyming Riddles

1. Have students think of as many words that rhyme with *bed* as they can. Have them tell their words to partners.

2. Distribute *The Monster Under My Bed Rhyming Riddles* (page 129) to students and make connections between the words students come up with in Step 1 with the words in the Word Bank.

3. Instruct students to use the words from the Word Bank to complete the riddles. Students can also create their own riddles for the words from the Word Bank or from the list of words they came up with in Step 1.

4. Have students illustrate one of the rhyming riddles on the backs of their papers.

Writing Connection

1. Have students read the poem again, paying particular attention to the final stanza. Have them write about what will happen next.

2. Have students share their predictions with the class.

Reader's Theater

1. Distribute *The Monster Under My Bed Reader's Theater* script (pages 130–133) to students.

2. Allow students to read the script independently.

3. Discuss the script.

4. Assign parts for five readers.

5. Allow several rehearsals to practice fluency.

6. Perform the reader's theater for the class, another class, or for a special school event.

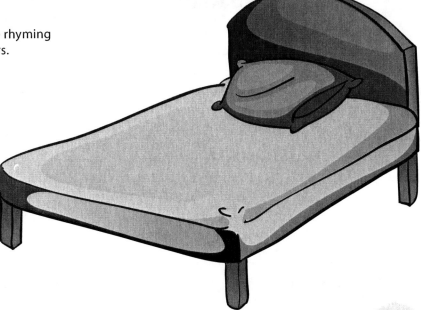

The Monster Under My Bed

by Karen McGuigan Brothers

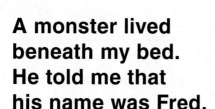

A monster lived
beneath my bed.
He told me that
his name was Fred.

I heard him move
around one night,
he tried his best
to give me fright.

But I just groaned
and then I sighed;
I was not scared,
although he tried.

He tried a "boo"
that was so weak,
I laughed so hard
I could not speak.

He tried again,
a bigger "boo,"
and then I said,
"What's wrong with you?"

"You could not scare
a scaredy cat
with a little
'boo' like that."

I told him he
should practice more
to turn his "boo"
into a roar.

He said he would
and so each night
I'd hear him "boo"
with all his might.

And when his "boo"
became a "BOOM"
I sneaked him to
my brother's room.

Name: _____ Date: _____

The Monster Under My Bed

Word Ladder

· ·

Directions: Listen to the clues. Then, write the words on the rungs below as you climb the ladder.

9.

8.

7.

6.

5.

4.

3.

2.

1.

The Monster Under My Bed

Closed Word Sort

Directions: Cut apart the cards. Then, sort them into groups according to the part of speech each represents: noun, verb, pronoun, adjective, or adverb. Refer to the poem to check how the words are used.

groaned	sighed	cat
lived	move	he
tried	laughed	I
speak	hear	you
said	sneaked	bigger
bed	brother	him
scare	hard	his
roar	monster	me
Fred	room	weak

Name: _____ Date: _____

The Monster Under My Bed

Rhyming Riddles

· ·

Directions: Use words from the Word Bank to complete the riddles below.
Note: You will not use all of the words.

Word Bank

sled	dead	tread
sped	bed	head
lead	red	thread

1. where the monster lived

a monster under a _____

2. a monster pretending he is not alive

a monster playing _____

3. a monster who is really angry

a monster seeing _____

4. a monster riding on snow

a monster on a _____

5. a monster who is going to sew

a monster with needle and _____

6. a monster with an itch

a monster scratching his _____

The Monster Under My Bed

Reader's Theater

All: The Monster Under My Bed

Reader 1:   A monster lived
beneath my bed.
He told me that
his name was Fred.

I heard him move
around one night,
he tried his best
to give me fright.

Reader 2:   I used to think there was a
monster living in my closet.

Reader 3:   What made you think that?

Reader 2:   I kept hearing a bumping noise against the closet door.

Reader 4:   Were you scared?

Reader 2:   I was very scared.

Reader 5:   What did you do?

Reader 2:   I mixed up some monster spray.

Reader 5:   Monster spray. What is monster spray?

Reader 2:   You mix up half a cup of water
with a teaspoon of cinnamon
and a couple of cloves. Then, you
put it in a spray bottle and shake
it up. I sprayed one quick spray
inside my closet before I went to bed.

The Monster Under My Bed

Reader's Theater *(cont.)*

Reader 3:   Did it work?

Reader 2:   It must have worked because I haven't heard any noises from my closet since.

Reader 4:   I thought I had a monster living in my closet once, but it was just the cat.

Reader 1:   Can we get back to the poem?

Readers 2–5:   Okay.

Reader 1:   I'll start again:

A monster lived
beneath my bed.
He told me that
his name was Fred.

I heard him move
around one night,
he did his best
to give me fright.

But I just groaned
and then I sighed.
I was not scared,
although he tried.

Reader 2:   You must be very brave.
I would have been
scared the minute I
heard a noise.

Reader 3:   I sleep with a flashlight
next to my bed. If I hear a
noise, I want to make sure it's
a monster before I start running and screaming.

The Monster Under My Bed

Reader's Theater *(cont.)*

Reader 4: But Fred sounds like a gentle monster. Read the rest of the poem.

Reader 1: Okay.

He tried a "boo"
that was so weak,
I laughed so hard
I could not speak.

He tried again,
a bigger "boo,"
and then I said,
"What's wrong with you?"

"You could not scare
a scaredy cat
with a little
'boo' like that."

Reader 2: Wow! You really were brave to actually talk to the monster like that!

Reader 3: It doesn't sound like a very scary monster to me. Scary monsters don't need help learning how to be scary.

The Monster Under My Bed

Reader's Theater *(cont.)*

Reader 1: Let me read the rest:

I told him he
should practice more
to turn his "boo"
into a roar.

He said he would
and so each night
I'd hear him "boo"
with all his might.

And when his "boo"
Became a "BOOM"
I sneaked him to
my brother's room.

Reader 4: Great idea! My brother
always tries to scare me.
He says he isn't afraid
of anything. I'd like to
sneak a monster into HIS room.

Reader 2: Then, you can sell him
some monster spray.

Tips for Implementing the Lessons

The Importance of Routines

Reading instruction needs to include a measure of predictability through activities that students do at regular times in their language arts classroom. Routines allow students to become self-directed learners because once they learn the routine, they do not have to rely on the teacher for directions for what to do next. This increases students' learning time and decreases teachers' planning time (Rasinski and Padak 2013; Rasinski, Padak, and Fawcett 2010).

Each lesson in this book follows a routine:

1. Introduction, Reading, and Rereading of the Rhyme
2. Word Work activities
   → *Word Ladder*
   → *Word Sort*
   → *Rhyming Riddles*
3. Writing Connection
4. Reader's Theater

The intention is not that you march sequentially through all the rhymes and activities in this book. Use the standards that accompany each lesson to guide you in selecting the rhymes and activities that your students need at any given time. Some standards may be addressed adequately in other instructional materials you use, while you may find some gaps in your curriculum that can be filled with activities in this book. In addition to the standards, stay attuned to what your students enjoy and learn from most.

Each lesson has multiple activities, so even if you eliminate a few, you will not be able to complete an entire lesson in one day. The following one-week routine can be adjusted according to the number of activities you decide to use. Another option is to learn the rhymes early in the year, revisit them regularly, and do an activity each time you revisit them.

Day	Task
Day 1	Introduce the rhyme to students.
Day 2	Reread the rhyme and complete one of the word work activities.
Day 3	Assign and practice the reader's theater script and complete a second word work activity.
Day 4	Practice the reader's theater script and complete the last word work activity.
Day 5	Perform the reader's theater script and complete the writing connection activity.

Tips for Implementing the Lessons *(cont.)*

Differentiation

We have been in education long enough to know that, despite frequent attempts at standardizing curriculum, instruction, and assessment, there is no such thing as a "standardized" child. Children in our schools come with great differences in abilities, background experiences, and motivation to learn.

As we stated before, you have the option to choose which activities are right for your students. Offer guidance as necessary to those who need additional help with specific activities.

Poetry Notebooks

Poetry Notebooks are an effective and engaging way to help students learn to recognize the form and sound of poetry. After the initial introduction of a poem or rhyme, students are given copies of it that they illustrate and add to three-ring binders.

Throughout the year, students enjoy browsing their poetry notebooks during sustained silent reading, reading poems with a partner during independent reading time, and sharing the poems with family and friends. A table of contents will help students locate their favorites. Some teachers add a "Lucky Listener" sheet to the front of the poetry notebook. Students take the notebooks home on a regular basis, and anyone they read to signs the sheet and makes comments if they wish. Some children even read to their pets and sign it themselves ("Good job! Love, Goldie") or make a paw print in the signature space. Below are examples of how students can create their own table of contents and Lucky Listener sheets. To help your students create poetry notebooks, see pages 137–139 for the *My Poetry Notebook* cover, the *Table of Contents*, and the *Lucky Listener* page.

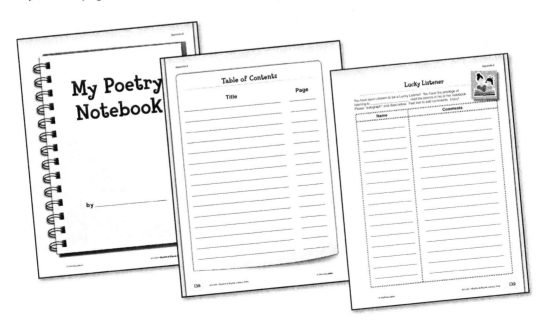

Name: _____ Date: _____

My Rhyming Words

Words that rhyme with _____

_____   _____

_____   _____

_____   _____

_____   _____

_____   _____

_____   _____

_____   _____

_____   _____

_____   _____

_____   _____

My Poetry Notebook

by _____

Table of Contents

Title	Page
_____	_____
_____	_____
_____	_____
_____	_____
_____	_____
_____	_____
_____	_____
_____	_____
_____	_____
_____	_____
_____	_____
_____	_____

Lucky Listener

You have been chosen to be a Lucky Listener! You have the privilege of listening to _____ read the poems in his or her notebook. Please "autograph" below. Feel free to add comments. Enjoy!

Name	Comments
_____	_____
_____	_____
_____	_____
_____	_____
_____	_____
_____	_____
_____	_____
_____	_____
_____	_____
_____	_____
_____	_____

Standards Correlations

Shell Education is committed to producing educational materials that are research and standards based. In this effort, we have correlated all of our products to the academic standards of all 50 states, the District of Columbia, the Department of Defense Dependents Schools, and all Canadian provinces.

How to Find Standards Correlations

To print a customized correlation report of this product for your state, visit our website at http://www.shelleducation.com and follow the on-screen directions. If you require assistance in printing correlation reports, please contact our Customer Service Department at 1-877-777-3450.

Purpose and Intent of Standards

Legislation mandates that all states adopt academic standards that identify the skills students will learn in kindergarten through grade twelve. Many states also have standards for Pre–K. This same legislation sets requirements to ensure the standards are detailed and comprehensive.

Standards are designed to focus instruction and guide adoption of curricula. Standards are statements that describe the criteria necessary for students to meet specific academic goals. They define the knowledge, skills, and content students should acquire at each level. Standards are also used to develop standardized tests to evaluate students' academic progress. Teachers are required to demonstrate how their lessons meet state standards. State standards are used in the development of all of our products, so educators can be assured they meet the academic requirements of each state.

Common Core State Standards

The activities in this book are aligned to the Common Core State Standards (CCSS). The chart on pages 141–142 lists the standards addressed in each lesson. Specific standards are also listed on the first page of each lesson.

TESOL and WIDA Standards

The activities in this book promote English language development for English language learners. The following TESOL and WIDA standards are addressed through the activities in this book:

◎ **Standard 1:** English language learners **communicate** for **social**, **intercultural**, and **instructional** purposes within the school setting.

◎ **Standard 2:** English language learners **communicate** information, ideas, and concepts necessary for academic success in the area of **language arts**.

Standards Correlations *(cont.)*

Standards that are specific to lessons are included on the first pages of the lessons and in the chart below. Standards that fit every lesson are listed below and indicate All Lessons. They are not always indicated on the first pages of the lessons.

Standard	Lessons
Literacy.L.3.1.a—Explain the function of nouns, pronouns, verbs, adjectives, and adverbs in general and their functions in particular sentences.	Peter Piper (p. 117); The Monster Under My Bed (p. 124)
Literacy.L.3.4.d—Use glossaries or beginning dictionaries, both print and digital, to determine or clarify the precise meaning of key words and phrases.	Pease Porridge Hot (p. 35); Little Miss Muffet (p. 53); Old Mother Hubbard (p. 86); Miss Mary Mack (p. 110); Peter Piper (p. 117)
Literacy.L.3.6—Acquire and use accurately grade-appropriate conversational, general academic, and domain-specific words and phrases, including those that signal spatial and temporal relationships.	Hickory Dickory Dock (p. 44)
Literacy.RF.3.3—Know and apply grade-level phonics and word analysis skills in decoding words.	All Lessons
Literacy.RF.3.3.c—Decode multi-syllable words.	Lock and Key (p. 62); Little Bo Peep (p. 70)
Literacy.RF.3.3.d—Read grade-level appropriate irregularly spelled words.	The Monster Under My Bed (p. 124)
Literacy.RF.3.4.a—Read with sufficient accuracy and fluency to support comprehension.	All Lessons
Literacy.RF.3.4.b—Read on-level prose and poetry orally with accuracy, appropriate rate, and expression on successive readings.	All Lessons
Literacy.RF.3.4.c—Use context to confirm or self-correct word recognition and understanding, rereading as necessary.	All Lessons
Literacy.RI.3.5—Use text features and search tools to locate information relevant to a given topic efficiently.	Jack Sprat (p. 9)
Literacy.RI.3.6—Distinguish their own point of view from that of the narrator or those of the characters.	Jack Sprat (p. 9)
Literacy.RL.3.1—Ask and answer questions to demonstrate understanding of a text, referring explicitly to the text as the basis for the answers.	All Lessons
Literacy.RL.3.4—Determine the meaning of words and phrases as they are used in a text, distinguishing literal from non-literal language.	Old Mother Hubbard (p. 86)
Literacy.RL.3.5—Refer to parts of stories, drama, and poems when writing or speaking about a text, using terms such as chapter, scene, and stanza; describe how each successive part builds on earlier sections.	Jack Sprat (p. 9); Sing a Song of Sixpence (p. 26); Pease Porridge Hot (p. 35); Me for Class President (p. 79); Old Mother Hubbard (p. 86)

Standards Correlations *(cont.)*

Standard	Lessons
Literacy.RL.3.10—By the end of the year, read and comprehend literature, including stories, drama, and poetry at the high end of the grades 2-3 text complexity band independently and proficiently.	All Lessons
Literacy.SL.3.2—Determine the main ideas and supporting details of a text read aloud or information presented in diverse media and formats, including visually, quantitatively, and orally.	For Want of a Nail (p. 95); Anna Maria (p. 103)
Literacy.SL.3.5—Create engaging audio recordings of stories or poems that demonstrate fluid reading at an understandable pace.	Lock and Key (p. 62); Little Bo Peep (p. 70); Me for Class President (p. 79); Peter Piper (p. 117)
Literacy.W.3.1—Write opinion pieces on topics or texts, supporting a point of view with reasons. Provide reasons that support the opinion.	Going to St. Ives (p. 17)
Literacy.W.3.3—Write narratives to develop real or imagined experiences or events using effective technique, descriptive details, and clear event sequences.	For Want of a Nail (p. 95); The Monster Under My Bed (p. 124)
Literacy.W.3.3.b—Use dialogue and descriptions of actions, thoughts, and feelings to develop experiences and events to show the response of characters to situations.	Little Miss Muffet (p. 53)
Literacy.W.3.5—With guidance and support from peers and adults, develop and strengthen writing as needed by planning, revising, and editing.	All Lessons
Literacy.W.4.4—Produce writing in which the development and organization are appropriate to task and purpose. (Grade 4)	Sing a Song of Sixpence (p. 26)
Literacy.W.3.10—Write routinely over extended time frames (time for research, reflection, and revision) and shorter time frames (a single setting or a day or two) for a range of discipline-specific tasks, purposes, and audiences.	All Lessons

References Cited

Adams, Marilyn J. 1990. *Beginning to Read: Thinking and Learning About Print*. Cambridge, MA: MIT Press.

Ball, Eileen, and Benita A. Blachman. 1991. "Does Phoneme Awareness Training in Kindergarten Make a Difference in Early Word Recognition and Developmental Spelling?" *Reading Research Quarterly* 26: 49–66.

Bromley, Karen. 2007. "Nine Things Every Teacher Should Know About Words and Vocabulary Instruction." *Journal of Adolescent and Adult Literacy* 50: 528–537.

Bryant, Peter E., Lynette Bradley, Morag Maclean, and Jennifer Crossland. 1989. "Nursery Rhymes, Phonological Skills, and Reading." *Journal of Child Language* 16 (2): 407–428.

Chall, Jeanne. 1983. *Stages of Reading Development*. New York, NY: McGraw Hill.

Denman, Gregory A. 1988. *When You've Made it Your Own: Teaching Poetry to Young People*. Portsmouth, NH: Heinemann.

Dowhower, Sarah L. 1987. "Effects of Repeated Reading on Second-Grade Transitional Readers' Fluency and Comprehension." *Reading Research Quarterly* 22: 389–407.

———. 1997. "The Method of Repeated Readings." *The Reading Teacher* 50: 376.

Dunst, Carl, Diana Meter, and Deborah W. Hornby. 2011. "Relationship Between Young Children's Nursery Rhyme Experiences and Knowledge and Phonological and Print-Related Abilities." *Center for Early Literacy Learning* 4: 1–12.

Gill, Sharon R. 2011. "The Forgotten Genre of Children's Poetry." *The Reading Teacher* 60: 622–625.

Griffith, Priscilla L., and Janell P. Klesius. 1990. "The Effect of Phonemic Awareness Ability and Reading Instructional Approach on First Grade Children's Acquisition of Spelling and Decoding Skills." Paper presented at the annual meeting of the National Reading Conference, Miami, FL.

Hackett, Kelly. 2013. *Ready! Set! Go! Literacy Centers*. Huntington Beach, CA: Shell Education.

Iwasaki, Becky, Timothy V. Rasinski, Kasim Yildirim, and Belinda S. Zimmerman. 2013. "Let's Bring Back the Magic of Song for Teaching Reading." *The Reading Teacher* 67: 137–141.

Maclean, Morag, Peter Bryant, and Lynette Bradley. 1987. "Rhymes, Nursery Rhymes, and Reading in Early Childhood." *Merrill Palmer Quarterly* 33: 255–281.

National Reading Panel. 2000. "Report of the National Reading Panel: Teaching Children to Read." Report of the subgroups. Washington, DC: U.S. Department of Health and Human Services, National Institutes of Health.

Perfect, Kathy A. 1999. "Rhyme and Reason: Poetry for the Heart and Head." *The Reading Teacher* 5: 728–737.

Rasinski, Timothy V., and Nancy D. Padak. 2013. *From Phonics to Fluency: Effective Teaching of Decoding and Reading Fluency in the Elementary School*. Boston, MA: Pearson.

References Cited *(cont.)*

Rasinski, Timothy V., Nancy D. Padak, and Gay Fawcett. 2010. *Teaching Children Who Find Reading Difficult,* 4th ed. Boston, MA: Pearson.

Rasinski, Timothy V., Nancy D. Padak, Elizabeth Sturtevant, and Wayne Linek. 1994. "Effects of Fluency Development on Urban Second-Grade Readers." *Journal of Educational Research* 87: 158–165.

Rasinski, Timothy V., William H. Rupley, and William D. Nichols. 2008. "Two Essential Ingredients: Phonics and Fluency Getting to Know Each Other." *The Reading Teacher* 62: 257–260.

———. 2012. *Phonics and Fluency Practice with Poetry.* New York: Scholastic.

Rasinski, Timothy V., and Belinda Zimmerman. 2013. "What's the Perfect Text for Struggling Readers? Try Poetry!" *Reading Today* 30: 15–16.

Samuels, S. Jay. 1997. "The Method of Repeated Readings." *The Reading Teacher* 50: 376–381.

Seitz, Sheila K. 2013. "Poetic Fluency." *The Reading Teacher* 67: 312–14.

Stahl, Steven A. 2003. "Vocabulary and Readability: How Knowing Word Meanings Affects Comprehension." *Topics in Language Disorders* 23 (3): 241–248.

Stahl, Steven A., and Kathleen M. Heubach. 2005. "Fluency-Oriented Reading Instruction." *Journal of Literacy Research* 37: 25–60.

Stanovich, Keith E. 1994. "Romance and Reason." *The Reading Teacher* 49: 280–291.

Templeton, Shane, and Donald Bear. 2011. "Teaching Phonemic Awareness, Spelling, and Word Recognition." In *Rebuilding the Foundation: Effective Reading Instruction for the 21st Century,* edited by Timothy Rasinski, 1–10. Bloomington, IN: Solution Tree.

Zimmerman, Belinda, and Timothy V. Rasinski. 2012. "The Fluency Development Lesson: A Model of Authentic and Effective Fluency Instruction." In *Fluency Instruction* 2nd ed., edited by Timothy V. Rasinski, Camille Blachowicz, and Kristin Lems, 172–184. New York, NY: Guilford.

Zimmerman, Belinda, Timothy V. Rasinski, and Maria Melewski. 2013. "When Kids Can't Read, What a Focus on Fluency Can Do." In *Advanced Literacy Practices: From the Clinic to the Classroom,* edited by Evan Ortlieb and Earl H. Cheek, 137–160. Bingley, UK: Emerald Group Publishing.